"This Isn't the Company I Joined"

Seven Steps to Energizing
a Restructured Work Force

Other titles of interest:

*Profit from Experience: The National Semiconductor Story
of Transformation Management*
Gil Amelio and William Simon

Leadership is Common Sense
Herman Cain

*Agile Competitors and Virtual Organizations:
Strategies for Enriching the Customer*
Steven L. Goldman, Roger N. Nagel, Kenneth Preiss

*One Size Fits One: Building Relationships One Customer
and One Employee at a Time*
Gary Heil, Tom Parker, Deborah C. Stephens

Presentations for Decision Makers
Marya W. Holcombe and Judith K. Stein

*Corporate Instinct: Building a Knowing Enterprise
for the 21st Century*
Thomas Koulopoulos, Robert Spinello, Wayne Toms

*Lasting Change: The Shared Values Process that Makes
Companies Great*
Rob Lebow and William Simon

*The Shape Shifters: Continuous Change for
Competitive Advantage*
John L. Mariotti

*Cooperate to Compete: Building Agile
Business Relationships*
Kenneth Preiss, Steven L. Goldman, Roger N. Nagel

"This Isn't the Company I Joined"

Seven Steps to Energizing a Restructured Work Force

Carol Kinsey Goman

JOHN WILEY & SONS, INC.

New York   Chichester   Weinheim   Brisbane   Singapore   Toronto

Copyright © 1998 by Carol Kinsey Goman

Published simultaneously in Canada.

This publication is designed to provide accurate and authoritative information in regard to the subject matter covered. It is sold with the understanding that the publisher is not engaged in rendering legal, accounting, or other professional services. If legal advice or other expert assistance is required, the services of a competent professional person should be sought.

2 3 4 5 6 7 8 9 10 QEBFF 01 00 99 98 97

Library of Congress Cataloging-in-Publication Data

Goman, Carol Kinsey.
    This isn't the company I joined: energizing a restructured work force / by
Carol Kinsey Goman.
        p.   cm.
    Includes index.
    ISBN 0-471-29262-1
    1. Organizational change.   2. Corporate reorganizations.   3. Organizational
behavior.   I. Title.
HD58.8.G653   1997   97-33631
658.4'063—dc21   CIP

To the Goman girls:
Belle, Wendy, Julie, Kim, Jennifer

. . . who embody the miracle inherent in all living systems.
They have transformed themselves into beautiful, loving, and
accomplished women.

ACKNOWLEDGMENTS

During the writing of this book, I received assistance from countless individuals and organizations around the world. Members of the International Association of Business Communicators deserve special mention for their unfailing generosity and support.

To my favorite writer and editor, George Kimball, I owe a deep debt of gratitude. This book is a collaborative effort and could not have been written without his significant contribution.

To my agent, Andrew Rock, and to Noah Shachtman, my editor at Van Nostrand Reinhold, I extend my heartfelt thanks for all their efforts on my behalf.

And to my husband, Ray K. Goman, who loved and tolerated me throughout the writing process, I can finally answer "Yes!" to his question, "Aren't you *ever* coming out of your office?"

CONTENTS

Chapter Four—Is the Change Finally Over?

Chapter Five—How Can I Take Control If You Keep Holding On?

Chapter Six—I'll Never Love a Company That Can't Love Me Back.

Chapter Seven—This Isn't the Company I Joined . . . It's Better!

The latest restructuring is completed. Employees feel secure again, satisfied that this change was necessary and for the best. All departments are back working at top capacity. The boardroom is viewed as credible, trustworthy, and inspired. Management is seen as caring and aware. You can relax in the knowledge that your part in leading the changeover has been a resounding success.

Right?

Not likely.

A more credible scenario finds the restructured work force feeling confused, demoralized, and deeply skeptical—fed up with being shuffled yet again like an old pack of cards and not at all convinced that this latest change was either necessary or useful in solving the company's current problems or meeting future demands. After all, weren't quality circles, teamwork, total quality movement (TQM) and previous restructuring all heralded as *the* solution? Weren't last year's goals the answer to everyone's prayers? Employees are now wondering whether the boardroom has any idea where this organization is headed, and management is seen as hopelessly out of touch with what's happening on the front lines.

As a leader of change your work has just begun.

Over the past 12 years, I have presented hundreds of speeches and seminars to corporate clients on the "human side" of organizational change. I always begin my addresses with a series of questions about the kinds of changes audience members are currently facing and about the psychological impact those changes are having on their own and their colleagues' morale. When I've collected enough answers to get a feel for the corporation's overall state of mind, I ask one final question: "How many of you have noticed that the company you are presently working for is not the company you joined?" The reply is always the same. After a moment's thought, hands begin shooting up all over the conference room as audience members realize that even if they started their jobs yesterday, something about the organization has already changed by today.

The New Reality

The past few years have witnessed unprecedented upheaval in the business world. Radically shifting marketplace dynamics, the rise of global competition, the advent of new technologies, a veritable revolution in consumer expectations and demands have combined to throw previously rock-solid business philosophies into a state of flux so extreme that many of today's corporate leaders, panicked into survival mode, are beginning to grasp at any promising straw in sight. "It worked for GE, it'll work for us." "It saved Citicorp's bacon, it'll damn well save ours." Only it almost never does. Too often, things get worse rather than better. The company starts to flounder, work force commitment declines, customers begin defecting to the competition. Why? Because 9 times out of 10 the latest rescue package is based on a business model that no longer corresponds to current business dynamics.

"The changes you're experiencing today aren't temporary aberrations," I always tell my management audiences. "They're real, they're fundamental and they're here to stay. You will never again reshape a company or manage a work force as you did in the good old days of stable corporate paradigms and predictable employee reactions. However brilliantly you may improvise, solutions to the challenges confronting you today cannot be constructed using the business models you grew up with. Those models no longer reflect reality. Stability is a thing of the past. Change *is* the new reality."

And there lies the "human" dilemma that business leaders face today: the need to energize employees in what has become a fundamentally unstable business environment.

The Employees' Perspective

"Think you're confused?" I tell my management audiences. "Try to imagine how *they* feel."

Lost is the short answer, with something about a creek and a missing paddle tagged on for emphasis. In fact, it's little wonder the work force feels disoriented today. Little wonder that declining morale, rising cynicism, and downright hostility are being reported more and more frequently at all levels of employment. Workers don't know where they stand anymore. They don't know what their companies are doing, and they aren't being told what their roles within their companies are supposed to be. As corporate policymakers thrash around seeking answers to the new facts of global business life, more and more workers find themselves being thrust willy-nilly into unfamiliar jobs that involve responsibilities they never agreed to undertake and the exercise of skills they never claimed to possess. Individualists are forged into teams and told to cooperate. Technicians are instructed to hone their "people skills." Employees at all levels are ordered to reengineer their jobs to meet the latest company demands, not understanding what those demands are and fearing that in the process they may make themselves redundant. Job security is disappearing. Benefits are being cut. Salaries are falling. Stress levels and workloads are rising. Everything is changing but no one's saying why.

From the employee's perspective, change itself isn't the

problem. The problem for employees is leadership. The work force can live with change. Employees can adapt and even thrive on change—*if* the change makes sense to them. That is the challenge business leaders face today. They need to make uncertainty comprehensible, to dispel anxiety, and to help employees see the potential inherent in the constantly fluctuating circumstances that have become the status quo of modern business's dynamics.

Creating involved, "change-adept" employees for the new business age won't be an easy task. Leaders will need to rethink a lot of outmoded "truths." This book points out the seven steps leaders can take in an effort to energize a restructured work force. They will need to learn new management strategies based on ideas about human resources that may never have occurred to them before. They will have to abandon the old corporate paradigms and accept the fact that business today is a whole new kind of ball game. And above all, they will have to find means to bring the work force as individuals, as human beings, back to the center of corporate strategy—because corporate survival in this chaotic, ever-changing, new business world of ours is going to rely crucially on the commitment, enthusiasm, talent, and creative contributions of every single employee from top to bottom of the organization.

"I'm not suggesting it will be easy," I tell my audiences, "But it can be done. It has to be done."

How to do it is what this book is about.

1

How Can I Play the Game When the Rules Keep Changing?

First Step: Examine Changing Realities

Five fundamental events created the new business dynamic that all companies and their employees must come to terms with today:

- The shift from domestic to global competition
- The shift from manpower to technopower
- The shift from company-led to consumer-driven market forces
- The shift from manufacturing to service-dominated economics
- The demographic transformation of the work force and the resulting shift in employer/employee relations

These five changes all occurred in the last 25–30 years. They are the defining events of the post-industrial age, and together they turned a once predictable landscape into a place where constant instability is the only "certainty." They also created the need for a new paradigm on which to base corporate decision making at all organizational levels. This chapter and the next examine the impact of these changes on business practices and consider the new paradigm they made necessary. The background they provide is essential to your understanding of the challenges organizations are facing today. Once you absorb the background, you'll be ready for the important task of mobilizing loyal, well-focused, and fully energized employees for the new business age.

GLOBALIZATION

For all practical purposes, all business today is global. Those individual businesses, firms, industries, and whole societies that clearly understand the new rules of doing business in a world economy will prosper; those that do not will perish.

Ira Mitroff, Professor, University
of Southern California

Prior to World War II, the number of U.S. firms involved in foreign investment was relatively small. Even after the war, most U.S. business activity remained centered on its domestic markets—markets that continued to provide adequate scope for growth and a natural competitive monopoly. Foreign imports were insignificant through the 1950s, and the products the United States exported were the same products it sold at home, shipped abroad without alteration or sensitivity to cultural differences.

Then, in the 1960s, this period of economic and cultural isolationism ended as relaxed tariff policies allowed cheaper foreign imports to compete seriously with domestic goods in a rapidly expanding consumer economy, and OPEC (oil and petroleum exporting countries), with its newfound petropower, began forcing U.S. industry and U.S. drivers into a painful readjustment of their thinking about fuel costs. At the same time, the cultural horizons of the United States began to broaden. Television brought the war in Vietnam into the nation's living rooms—often on sets made by Vietnam's neighbors—and U.S.

citizens started traveling abroad in large numbers for the first time. By the 1980s, with the birth of the Asian Tigers and the opening of lucrative new markets in Europe, the Middle East, and Africa, U.S. business suddenly realized that it had some serious catching up to do in the areas of product design, quality, marketing, and overseas service if it wanted to compete successfully with its more experienced foreign opposition in the new global arena.

Today, the United States has become a front-line player in that arena: a major force in multinational production, worldwide distribution, and global strategic alliance. In an age when daily foreign exchange volume is $1.3 trillion and U.S. corporations are directly investing more than $100 billion a year in international markets, the majority of the largest U.S. companies now conduct more of their business activities abroad than they do at home. U.S. exports have increased more than 10 times in the last two decades, and of the 1,000 largest industrial corporations in the United States, 700 expect their international growth to exceed their domestic growth in the next five years.

But globalization isn't a one-way street. Overseas goods, services, ideas, and personnel are pouring into the United States just as quickly as they are being shipped out. Even small businesses now compete with and have access to products, labor, and new marketing techniques from all over the world. Competitors are no longer located just down the block. They are based in Malaysia and Chile and Finland and South Africa. The same holds true for work forces. Employee pools, once thought of as geographically static, now migrate across international borders as easily as cars or computer chips. Companies can locate—or relocate—where the tax laws are most advantageous and where skilled, cost-effective labor is most readily available. Workloads can be spread over several time zones to cut production costs and facilitate delivery schedules. Individual technicians can go wherever their expertise is needed. Quality control and new product design, once domestically determined, now

meet international standards as a matter of course. New recruits are trained specifically for overseas service. The fact is
that all aspects of business are internationalized today. The
truly global company is a nonnational company—one that is
culturally neutral and regards all nations as equally important
to its prosperity. The easy movement of money and people
across borders, the creation of multinational alliances and
strategies, the revolution in information technology, and the
convergence of foreign cultures and markets combined to turn
the world into one huge shopping mall.

However, globalization is an executive-led phenomenon.
The work force played no direct role in its development, and
most employees have little understanding of its dynamics. Because this lack of understanding can lead to confusion and even
a collapse of commitment, it is the leader's job to make sure
that people throughout the organization are fully informed
about the company's global future and about how each fits personally into that future.

Here are some concrete strategies to help you accomplish
that aim:

• Communicate your global mission and goals so that employees get used to thinking of the organization in an international context. Announce your international standings and
revenues, talk about global challenges and opportunities region
by region, and explain how your various overseas locations support one another and contribute to corporate objectives.

• Include news of international activity in all organizational
communications—from employee newsletters to speeches from
senior management. Discuss the ways in which trends, events,
treaties, currency fluctuations, and laws around the world affect the organization.

• Offer courses in how to do business in other countries. Invite all employees to attend.

• Encourage employees to learn a second (or third) language. Acknowledge and reward them for acquiring these additional language skills.

- At company meetings, bring in speakers from other global organizations and ask for their views on the impact of globalization on their businesses. Invite overseas managers from your organization to make presentations in the United States. Encourage repatriated employees to describe their experiences abroad.

- Review organizational policies on recruiting, training, and relocating employees to make sure there is a global emphasis.

- Reward employees with trips abroad to attend international conferences, to visit your facility in another country, or to meet with customers in other countries.

THE TECHNOLOGICAL REVOLUTION

The Third Wave sector includes not only high-flying computer and electronic firms or biotech start-ups. It embraces advanced information-driven manufacturing in every industry. It includes the increasingly data-drenched services—finance, software, entertainment, the media, advanced communications, medical services, consulting, training, and education—in short, all the industries based on mind-work rather than muscle-work.

Alvin Toffler, Futurist and Author

Advances in technology drive change throughout organizations, enabling them to improve their business processes by replacing routine activities with information systems and robotics. Instant electronic transmission makes it possible to move data entry jobs to any location on the globe. Advances in electronic networking are redistributing power in organizations, making it feasible for employees to skip levels in the chain of command, providing senior executives with direct access to employee feedback on performance and organizational issues, and making workers at remote sites feel that they are part of the team.

In the United States, 25 million people are currently linked to the Internet and can instantly share sound, data, and images from any place on the globe. Estimates are that a billion people worldwide will have Internet access by the year 2000. Intranets (internal computer networks that rely on the same information systems technology as the World Wide Web) are becoming the new pathways to the intelligence of the organization. These networks give people in different departments access to one another and offer instant access to the same information to employees around the world. Intranet systems allow organizations to capture and share knowledge throughout the organization, to exchange best practices and good ideas companywide, and to reinforce the corporate culture.

"As new computer systems decentralize control and empower people all along the information chain, they dissolve conventions of ownership, design, manufacturing, executive style, and national identity," writes George Gilder in the *Harvard Business Review*. To illustrate his point, Gilder describes the Brooktree Company, inventor of RAM-DAC and related devices that convert digital video information for analog display or analog images for digital manipulation, windowing, panning, editing, and zooming. Explains Gilder, "Brooktree is not a hierarchy but an information heterarchy, with multiple centers of power and hundreds of online workstations around the globe. The company has no one factory of its own but links its process technology with any number of major chip fabricators around the world. Its devices are made in Japan or the United States, packaged in Korea, and burned-in and tested in San Diego."

Technology provides employees with direct access to information necessary for business decisions. This transfer of knowledge directly to workers has made possible—and inevitable—many of the changes in the organizational structure of the corporation and is one of the major forces behind increasing employee empowerment.

That is the good news. The downside, of course, is the loss of jobs. Automated teller machines, robots, and electronic voice mail replace human bank tellers, assembly-line workers, and telephone operators who all used to collect paychecks and are now collecting unemployment. Walter Wriston, the former chairman and chief executive officer (CEO) of Citicorp, draws a parallel between the current shift into the "information age" and the previous transformation of the agricultural society to an industrial one:

> A close-eyed view of the world would reveal that the old industrial world is fading and being replaced by a new information society. This transformation does not mean that manufacturing doesn't matter, or that it is not important, or that it will disappear, any more than the advent of the industrial age meant that agriculture disappeared. What it does mean is that, like agriculture today, manufacturing will produce more goods for more people with less labor.

In their book, *The One to One Future,* authors Don Peppers and Martha Rogers use this example to illustrate how technology affects workers:

> When one of the first steam shovels went into use, a story is told about the union boss who confronted the construction company president with a demand that he stop using the machine as it would put several dozen laborers out of work. He wanted the construction company to agree to continue using work crews with shovels. In response, the executive offered to eliminate the shovel, too, and replace it with a teaspoon—to provide even more jobs.

Technological progress is inevitable, and new technology inevitably displaces workers. But the most important thing to those employees who no longer dig ditches by hand or take orders by telephone is to know that they can learn the skills needed to survive in this changing business world. Human nature drives employees to resist implementing technological change until they are shown how the technology enables them to do their jobs better, faster, more easily, and how cross-training for new high-tech functions can mean brighter, more secure futures for themselves and their families.

CUSTOMER POWER

In India, we refer to customers as "The emperors of choice."

K. M. Mammen, Vice Chairman and
Managing Director, M.R.F. Ltd.

Consumers are becoming relentless in their demands for quality, service, customization, convenience, speed, and competitive pricing. And with global competition and the new technologies providing customers ever greater choice about when, how, and where they will receive goods and services, they have, in effect, become *the* determining factor in the success or failure of most companies. We are selling products and services to an increasingly informed and sophisticated consumer today: a consumer no longer prepared to pay inflated prices for less than ideal goods because of their brand names or because no equivalent product is available. Today there is *always* an equivalent product available somewhere in the world—and customers ready to defect to the opposition if your version doesn't come up to their standards.

When Armstrong International Corporation first started selling steam traps in Japan, the company received complaints about how the traps looked. Appearance doesn't affect performance, of course, but because the Japanese expected no nicks, blemishes, or color distortions on their products, Armstrong immediately changed to a high-pigment paint that produced a richer-looking paint job and began shipping the traps in individual packing so they didn't bump against one another in transit. The Japanese renewed the contract and Armstrong saved a valuable customer at a cost of only a few cents per unit.

Marketing strategies as well as quality considerations have undergone similar transformation in ways ranging from packaging and logo design to televisions and print media advertising techniques. How products and services are sold to customers today is just as important as the products themselves. In the retail sector, leaders look for new ways to reach the new customer, targeting in particular the growing number of dual-income consumers who have more to spend but less time to shop. It is now commonplace to see 24-hour grocery stores, pharmacies, and laundromats. Gas stations sell food, supermarkets offer banking services, and banks let you do it all by phone. Perhaps the biggest change of all, though, is seen in the increase in access of direct sales into the home and business markets through catalogues, home shopping channels on television, and the Internet.

The new standard of excellence for all organizations today is meeting, or exceeding, customer expectations. To this end, companies are organizing around personnel with direct customer contact, encouraging customer critique and listening to their concerns, empowering employees to quickly satisfy customer demands, and involving customers in the process of developing new products and services. Jan Carlzon, former chairman of Scandinavian Airlines System (SAS), labeled every employee–customer interaction as a "moment of truth" and said that the quality of a customer's experience at each of these moments ultimately determined whether SAS succeeds or fails.

When Boeing invited customers to be a partner in the design process of the Boeing 777, it took a calculated risk. Boeing let customers see the inner workings of the company and in doing so risked exposing its shortcomings. Further, by inviting customers into the process, Boeing was soliciting customer opinions and suggestions when Boeing itself was supposed to be the expert. But the partnership worked extremely well because the result was a product that *fully* met customer needs and expectations.

As a leader, you promote the critical employee–customer relationship when you do the following:

- Invite a panel of customers to address employees and have the customers say what they like and don't like about your company's products/services.

- Send employees to your customer's place of business and let workers personally see the business challenges and problems that the customer faces.
- Use customer questionnaires and publish the results —both positive and negative. And when the negative comments point to a specific problem, create an employee–customer task force to investigate and solve it.
- Invite customers to attend strategy sessions and product development meetings.
- Publish every letter of praise or complaint that comes from customers.
- Make "heroes" out of workers who solve customers' problem in creative ways. Tell their stories in your speeches and other corporate communications.
- Create an "idea campaign" around the question "*How can we surprise and delight the customer?*"
- Send employees to trade shows that are also attended by customers.
- Base a portion of employees' pay on customer evaluations.

THE NEW SERVICE-DOMINATED ECONOMICS

Service isn't just a word in our corporate philosophy; it's the very reason Federal Express exists.

Federal Express *Manager's Guide*

Based on the latest gross domestic product figures, service industries of one kind or another now predominate over manufacturing in the United States by four to one. More than 8 out of 10 U.S. workers are employed somewhere in the service/information sector today. And customer service, once considered a retailing side issue, has now become a key factor in the marketing strategies of all survival-minded companies. The same is true abroad—so much so, in fact, that the International Monetary Fund dropped the label "industrialized countries" when referring to the world's developed nations, replacing it with the now more accurate term "advanced economies."

The shift from industrial to service-based business activity occurred with extraordinary swiftness in this country (in 1950, 73 percent of U.S. workers were still engaged in manufacturing and related occupations), and its impact on our thinking about work and the workplace is as profound as that experienced 100 years ago when the United States shifted from being an agricultural nation to being an industrial one. Only a generation ago, trained technical workers were a relative rarity in this country. By the year 2000, it is estimated they will comprise nearly a quarter of the total U.S. work force. The most highly skilled, the so-called knowledge workers, will be engaged in steadily more specialized activities, while the tasks demanding less rigorous education (technical and legal research, lab analysis, computer programming, etc.) will be handed over to a growing body of "paraprofessional" support workers whose roles in today's service/information world equate roughly to those carried out by the trained mechanics and quality-control engineers of the industrial age. Specialized subcontracting services in a variety of technical fields are also proliferating as such large professional organizations as hospitals, consulting companies, law firms, multinational publishers, and media conglomerates find that detailed work once done in-house can be done faster, more cost-effectively, and often better by independent specialists.

Outside the technical arena, more and more "people skill" jobs are also appearing—jobs ranging from customer relations and product/service follow-up to media-based sales and advice/help services of all kinds. Individual service jobs—housecleaning, child and elder care, janitorial work, gardening, home maintenance and repair, transport, even dog walking—are also increasing in number as dual-career families find less and less time to deal with domestic demands. The U.S. Bureau of Labor Statistics predicts personal service work will be one of the fastest-growing employment sectors in the twenty-first century.

According to the *Fortune* article "How We Will Work in the Year 2000," the main mind-set shift for companies will be a move from "thinking of business as making things to realizing that it consists instead of furnishing services, even within what is traditionally thought of as manufacturing." The article goes on to say that "much of the quality movement can be understood as building more service into a product. When an Eastman Kodak or Allied-Signal breaks down its operations into the steps by which it adds value, the company is really identifying the series of services performed that eventually lead to greater customer satisfaction."

Lord Rees-Mogg, former editor of the *London Times* said, "In the future, more businesses will be based on intangibles than on tangibles." And with that shift has come a whole new list of priorities and challenges in the management and training of a work force:

- Knowledge workers can't be bullied. (Have you ever tried getting heavy-handed with the technician who repairs the copy machine?)
- Today's top professionals demand to be kept at the top of their field. (Professional development is fast becoming a term of employment.)
- Employees who are expected to treat the customer extremely well must be treated extremely well by management. (As Walt Disney said, "You'll never have great customer relations until you have good employee relations.")

THE CHANGING WORK FORCE

Why can't they be like we were . . . perfect in every way?

From the song *Kids*

In fundamentally important ways, the work forces you are hiring today are not the work forces you would have hired only a generation ago. Less than 40 years separate the two groups. But the difference in philosophy, demographic makeup, social conditions, life experience, and individual expectations are already enormous. And they will continue to grow even larger as we move into the next millennium. Old perceptions can no longer be relied on to guide you in your management of employer–employee relations today. Of the changing realities being examined in this chapter, the philosophical and material transformation of the work force over the last four decades is the one that has the most critical impact on corporate survival in the new business age.

Work Force Philosophy

More than 43 million jobs have been erased in the United States since 1979, an inevitable result of progress into the new business age, but one that has had a profoundly negative effect on work force mentality. An accelerating erosion of morale and commitment is evident in recent years as employees at all levels of competency realize that downsizing, even in prosperous times, is a permanent weapon in the post-industrial corporate arsenal. Workers know they aren't being laid off today because of ineptitude, poor performance, or inadequate training. They're being laid off because their jobs can now be done more efficiently and less expensively by other means. According to the American Management Association, only 6 percent of the companies that downsized between mid-1994 and mid-1995 did so because of declining business. The rest cut employee numbers for strategic reasons unrelated to traditional labor–management issues—reasons that all point to the fact that a significant proportion of the old industrial-based work force simply isn't needed anymore. What the "downsized" are being forced to accept today is that unlike past layoffs caused by periodic dips in the business cycle, these new layoffs are probably permanent. That realization, coupled with the confusion caused by the shift to the new post-industrial economy, has created in several million intelligent, talented, potentially valuable employees a sense of deepening anxiety that is infecting not only themselves but the whole U.S. work force.

It isn't only the casualties of the new global economy who are suffering from work force angst today. The survivors may still have jobs to go to, but they also have eyes to see what has happened to their colleagues and instincts that keep sending out negative messages about their own futures in a changing workplace that is making more and more demands on them while providing less and less material and emotional satisfaction. A Roper Starch survey conducted in 1994 among a cross-section of U.S. employees (including professional and middle-management people) found that only 1 in 4 could claim to be more than marginally satisfied with his or her present job—a decline of nearly 40 percent from the response given only 20 years earlier. Only 43 percent of the workers questioned felt that they understood what was expected of them in their jobs. Only 39 percent had a clear idea of their company's aims. Nearly 1 in 3 feared they would be out of work within a year; 62 percent felt they were not respected by their bosses; 74 percent believed they were underpaid. And when asked about job satisfaction, only 4 in 10 could claim they derived any enjoyment from their work at all!

Those figures, plus the growing hopelessness seen in the ranks of the unemployed, define the predominant philosophical reality that managers are trying to cope with today: the collective philosophy of a skeptical, insecure, overstressed working population whose view of the future is, to put it mildly, bleak. Not a good reality for the new business age—and particularly not when one realizes how many of those disaffected workers are under the age of 35.

At present, the U.S. work force is still dominated statistically by baby boomers—76 million men and women born between 1946 and 1964, who began taking over the job market in the euphoric 1960s, survived two serious recessions in the 1970s and 1980s, and came out the other side knowing more about the ups and downs of "the American dream" than probably any other work force generation ever has. As a whole, the boomers are a tough-minded, hard-working, realistic bunch who learned from experience the importance of looking out for number one. But now a new generation of workers (Generation X, or Gen X) is feeding into the equation, 44 million relatively inexperienced 21 to 33-year-olds born after the 1960s, who would once have been thought of as America's future, but who are presently struggling to make space for themselves in a contracting job market so discouraging that they might better be described as America's forgotten. "This is a generation of diminished expectation," Laura Zinn wrote in a 1995 *Business Week* profile. "Polar opposites of the baby boomers who grew up thinking anything was possible. Far too many Gen-Xers have graduated straight out of high school or college into unemployment or underemployment," Zinn declares, and far too many, she goes on, are still there today, either existing on federal and state handouts or scraping by on the mundane, underpaid pickings that author Douglas Coupland calls "McJobs." The best educated and best prepared are doing okay, of course. But they are in the minority. According to the latest figures, Generation X now leads America's unemployment statistics by some 30 percent above the national average—a figure underlined by a 1994 Northeastern University market study which found that households headed by adults under 30 were 21 percent *less* well off in real dollar terms than the average equivalent household 20 years earlier.

That situation hasn't been experienced in the United States since the 1930s. And what experts fear is that the collective mind-set it is producing may result in one of the most difficult-to-manage and -motivate work force generations this country has ever known. That potential problem, added to the entrenched skepticism of the baby boomers, has to be dealt with right now. Loyal, contributive work forces cannot be built on mistrust and alienation. The present negative thinking has to be turned around. To do that, managers must understand, and be prepared to act constructively on, all the material and emotional conditions that define their employees' lives today.

It may be difficult to gauge the exact amount of skepticism, alienation, and mistrust that permeate your work force, but you *can* measure employee morale and job satisfaction—and when you find problem areas, you can address them openly.

Employee Morale Survey

1. On a five-point scale, where "1" is extremely dissatisfied and "5" is extremely satisfied, how satisfied are you with your present job?

2. On a five-point scale, where "1" is extremely dissatisfied and "5" is extremely satisfied, how satisfied are you with this organization?

3. On a five-point scale, where "1" is extremely low and "5" is extremely high, how would you rate the general level of employee morale?

4. Do you know what is expected of you on the job?

5. Do you know the long-term goals of the organization?

6. Does your supervisor respect you as a person?

7. Do you trust senior management to tell you the truth?

8. At work, do your opinions seem to count?

9. On a five-point scale, where "1" is extremely likely and "5" is extremely unlikely, how likely do you think it is that you be laid off within the next five years?

10. On a five-point scale, where "1" is totally out of touch and "5" is extremely in touch, how do you rate senior management's understanding of what employees think and feel about working here?

11. From your most objective viewpoint, are you compensated fairly for your work?

12. Would you recommend this company to your friends if they were seeking employment?

13. Are you actively seeking employment outside this company?

Springfield Remanufacturing Corporation is an organization that prides itself on its participative work practices and high employee morale. When Springfield Remanufacturing distributed a questionnaire to be answered anonymously by its work force, the responses "floored many of our managers," according to Jack Stack, the CEO. "The truth is, these types of morale problems are easy to miss, especially if you think you're doing well."

Demographics

Only 40 years ago, white adult males comprised 90 percent of the U.S. work force. Today, that figure has already changed dramatically, and in 10 years' time it will have changed even more. By the year 2007, the Bureau of Labor Statistics estimates that women and members of ethnic minorities will make up 62 percent of all workers in full- or part-time employment in the United States. Hispanics and African Americans of both sexes will each comprise about 11 percent, Asians of both sexes will account for roughly 5 percent, and of the total estimated work force of 151 million, white adult males will account for only 38 percent, a decrease of well over half since 1960.

Diversity is the new demographic reality in the U.S. work force. More women, more ethnic minorities, more complex demands—more urgent competition for jobs, too, as relaxed immigration policies see more foreign workers, both high-tech and unskilled, enter the country seeking livelihoods—all of which adds up to more work for managers. The companies that succeed in the next century will be the ones that become the most adept at attracting and retaining the best and the brightest from an employment "salad" that is also going to contain a steadily widening range of languages, customs, religious backgrounds, sexual orientations, domestic arrangements, and life experiences. Each group will bring its own special needs and agendas into the workplace, and to ignore any of them, or to show favoritism to one group over another, is to invite the alienation of all. Diversity, it's true, does bring a greater demand for managerial sensitivity. But it also brings new ideas, fresh perspectives, new energy sources, and new blood. Diversity, I tell my audiences, has to be treated as a positive. Because it *is* a positive. If the salad is causing trouble, introduce diversity programs into the company. Take concrete steps to understand, appreciate, and profit from the uniqueness around you. Get everyone involved and find what works. Or, as one manager put it: "Sensitivity training is all well and good, but it's just the first step. You've got to focus on how to turn diversity into a positive, competitive advantage."

• Link diversity with customer service. One obvious advantage of a diverse work force is its ability to understand and be more responsive to the needs of a diverse customer base.

• Capitalize on diversity in problem solving. People of all ages and from different backgrounds bring to the empowered workplace fresh ideas, opinions, perspectives, and boundless creativity. It is the richness of the diverse perspectives, used in solving real business problems, that gives a company the innovative edge.

• Make diversity an explicit value of the organization—and hold people accountable for honoring that value. Then put values into action; when the company offers diversity trainings, make sure that senior managers are the first to attend and to discuss their personal challenges.

• Position diversity not as a "feel good" issue but a business issue—the need to retain all talented employees.

• Sponsor organizational "associations" for various employee groups as an informal forum to express concerns, gain support, and share experiences.

• Make diversity an issue in management's evaluation and compensation. A corporate example is Xerox's "balanced work force strategy," in which senior managers are evaluated in part on their success in hiring, keeping, developing, and promoting minorities and women.

• Promote unity. Ultimately, the talents, abilities, and perspectives of a diverse employee population must be united toward a common organizational objective which challenges and rewards all who participate.

Age

The average work force age, presently 39.6 years, will continue to rise over the next decade until it peaks at about 40.5 years in 2005. Thereafter, age levels will fall again as Generation X and its successors replace retiring baby boomers. For the next 10 years, however, age is going to remain a not inconsiderable issue for managers and corporate executives.

By 2005, nearly 40 percent of the work force will be 45 or older, and one in three people over the age of 55 will still be in a job. Adding to the natural work force aging process over the next decade will be the fact that the trend toward early retirement in the 1970s and 1980s is now beginning to reverse. Abrupt cost-of-living increases coupled with salary squeezing, benefits cuts, and a sharp rise in the cost of private health care mean that older baby-boom workers who can go on working will do so as a matter of expediency.

Many managers fear that an aging work force is going to blunt their company's competitive edge: that older workers are less productive, less flexible in outlook, more resistant to structural innovation, and more expensive to keep. Not true, according to research carried out by the American Association of Retired Persons (AARP) in 1995. What AARP found, in fact, was that older workers worked just as hard, just as quickly, and often more economically than their juniors; that the experience and stability they brought to a work force actually encouraged productivity; that the job was what they wanted, not bigger salaries for longer service; and that generally speaking, they were more flexible about restructuring, part-time work, and odd-hour shifts than anyone would have imagined. So managers needn't worry about those problems. What they do need to worry about, however, is "clogging." The persistence of long-term workers in a numerically static work force means that there aren't enough employment opportunities for younger people coming up. Hence, we have all those Gen-X college graduates doing McJobs today. Managers must find some means to overcome that clogging now—through company training programs, job sharing, more part-time scheduling, apprentice-ships—anything that will make the new generation feel it has a legitimate stake in the company's and the nation's economic future.

Education

The work force of the future is going to be increasingly computer literate. But that is probably the only positive thing that can be said about its educational attainment. The public school system in the United States today is in a woeful state. Despite Generation X's high college graduate rate, U.S. schools are turning out future employees by the hundreds of thousands who can neither read well enough to understand a personnel manager's questionnaire nor write well enough to fill it in intelligibly. Surveys show that more and more young people are joining the work force each year without even a basic grounding in history, politics, arithmetic, or English grammar. It isn't a matter of declining intelligence. It's a matter of declining educational standards—and that goes for college as well as high school graduates. Blame for what's gone wrong with the once envied public education system can be laid at enough doorsteps to furnish a city block. But blame isn't the issue for business leaders. The issue is how best to train and motivate a growing work force that knows more about pop videos, computer games, and television soap operas than it does about self-discipline and basic learning skills.

The most forward-thinking of U.S. corporations, realizing that valuable talent can be lost by expecting too much educationally of new applicants, are already building educational shortfall factors into their recruitment policies. They assume automatically that the average new employee, however promising he or she may be, probably won't be educationally equipped to handle the special requirements of the job being offered. A number of these companies—most well-known among them Motorola—have therefore set up in-house, back-to-school training programs for their employees. The Motorola program is particularly successful. But even it had to be rethought after the first year because it seriously overestimated the education level of employees. According to William Wiggenhorn, vice president of training, a survey of employees at one Motorola division found that only 40 percent could pass an exam that included questions as simple as "10 is what percent of 100?" Other organizations, equally alert to the talent–learning discrepancy affecting the work force, are funding outside night-school classes as a basic part of their employment contracts. And, if the standard of public school education continues to fall in this country, these programs, radical at the moment, are soon going to become the norm for all survival-minded companies.

Family Structures

Your family may be nuclear, stable, well housed, and financially secure. But statistics show that less than half the families in the United States today can claim to match that profile, which means that more than half the men and women who make up today's work force are dealing on a daily basis with problems and life situations that you may never have experienced. And many of the changes have come so fast that business has not had time to adjust to them.

According to figures published in 1960, 54 percent of U.S. work force families were "traditional" in structure—a breadwinner father, a homemaker mother, and their 2.4 children under 18 years old. Dual-breadwinner families in 1960 accounted for only 26 percent of the total work force, single-parent breadwinner mothers numbered under 4 percent, single-parent breadwinner fathers counted for a scant 2 percent, and the remaining 14 percent of the work force was made up of one or more members from other family groupings (single children still living at home, unmarried couples, working wives, etc.). The annual divorce rate among 1960 work force families ran slightly below the national average at about 7.5 per 1,000, and the number of families where one or other adult was a stepparent averaged just over 6.8 per 1,000.

Ozzie and Harriet, it seems, really did mirror reality in 1960. But they wouldn't for much longer. By 1990, dual-breadwinner families rose in number to 44 percent of the total work force. Single-parent breadwinner mothers trebled to nearly 12 percent. Single-parent breadwinner fathers rose slightly to 3 percent, other family groupings accounted for 23 percent, and the traditional breadwinner father/homemaker mother family plummeted from more than half of the total work force in 1960 to less than 1 in 5 (18 percent) in 1990. Divorce rates, meanwhile, shot up to an annual 22 per 1,000 marriages, stepparent families rose to 21 per 1,000, and of all marriages in the United States in 1990, only 54.1 percent were first marriages for both partners. Exit Ozzie and Harriet, enter Roseanne, Frazier, and Grace Under Fire.

Clearly, and perhaps understandably, the traditional family structure was breaking down under the stress of post-industrial life in the United States. But the breakdown was not philosophically based. The importance of families as a necessary and desirable cultural institution remained as strong as ever. According to Joseph H. Coates, founder/editor of *The Futurist,* "It isn't the idea of what a family means that is changing today, it's the definition of what a family *is.*" In his 1996 study of work force family patterns, Coates found a wide variety of nontraditional family forms springing up in all regions of the United States to replace traditional ones.

These changes in the definition of what constitutes a family are going to play a critical role in shaping management practices of the future, not the least because so many of the traditional support roles of members of the old nuclear family will have to be played in the future by people and organizations from outside the family. As industrial psychologists have noted, the breakdown of the traditional family often leaves employees nowhere to turn for help with everyday problems other than their place of employment. A 1993 survey of Silicon Valley employees, nearly half of whom are unmarried, under 30, and often living too far from home to enjoy regular contact with parents and childhood friends, revealed that a majority looked to their companies for the sense of community and companionship that they would otherwise have sought in family structures. "At least they try to make you feel like you belong," one Silicon Valley exile admitted wistfully.

But it is the practical problems arising from family restructuring that companies are going to have to address most urgently in the future: accommodating less rigid work schedules for single parents, arranging time off for child- and elder-care responsibilities, making space in the organization for job sharing, permanent part-time employment, working from home options, and providing in-house counseling for problems ranging from mortgages to maternity counseling. "Flexibility at all levels," according to Jim Wall, director of human resources at Deloitte-Touche, "is going to be crucial to retaining good employees."

- Talk to employees one-on-one about their family issues.
- Tell the work force about your own efforts to balance work and family. Lew Platt, the CEO of Hewlett Packard, was a single father for several years after the death of his first wife. He uses examples from his personal life to show employees he understands the issues they face.
- Review the company's policies to see whether they are realistically "family friendly"—or whether they need to be updated to fit the current times. For example, have you structured management jobs so that they require a stay-at-home partner, just so all the activities of daily living can be taken care of?
- Explore "flexplace" work arrangements that utilize various combinations of "face" time in the office with time working from home.
- Provide personal leave policies that make it possible for employees to take time off work without an emergency and without jeopardizing their job security.
- Be realistic in what you promise. In a tough, competitive business, a company can't always make the job easier, but it can offer some flexibility in the way employees work.

Decision Making

Vietnam, Watergate, Travelgate, You-Name-It-Gate—as the list grows, the gullibility quotient in the United States shrinks in direct proportion. The nation is pretty skeptical about authority these days, and that skepticism is reflected in current work force attitudes toward corporate decision making and goal setting. Teamworking and other structural innovations in the 1980s and 1990s have gone some way to bring middle- and lower-echelon workers into the decision-making process. But expect employees in the future to demand an even greater say in how their companies set and execute goals, organize the work force, and distribute rewards. The growing individualism that already characterizes the present work force is going to become even more pronounced in the next century. The workplace is going to become more volatile, not less, as trust in authority declines and employees at all levels find the voice to express their own views. Managers may find managing more difficult as a result, but the best will discover means to turn those difficulties to their companies' and their workers' advantage by promoting greater commitment through greater participation.

The horizontal organization is one example of how the workplace is being structured to encourage employee participation. In the horizontal organization, we find the following:

- Teams provide the foundation of organizational design. They are not set up inside departments, like marketing, but around core processes, such as new product development.
- Work is organized around outcomes, not tasks. Employee teams have to make more decisions for themselves. Backed by adequate support and information technology, they are responsible for measurable results.
- Hierarchies are flattened and work is simplified by combining related tasks and eliminating work that does not add value.
- Functional pockets in the organization are created when needed in centers of excellence and technical pools or for such vertical-integrating processes as finance and strategy.
- The focus goes beyond just the financial goals or functional objectives and, instead, emphasizes building relationships with customers.

When it works right, the horizontal organization is the kind of company that employees themselves would design.

Employee Loyalty

They were raised by working parents who sacrificed family time for upward mobility, and they watched those parents being laid off by employers after 10/20/30 years of loyal service. Don't expect today's newest employees to sign up for the same deal. Although some members of the baby-boom work force may envy the "good old days" of lifetime employment security, that concept plays only a marginal role in the new workplace ethos of younger workers. Increasingly, employees are ready and all too willing to switch jobs if their present company doesn't fulfill their expectations. Post-baby boomers especially will become used to job hopping and periods of unemployment. They'll also be used to getting by on McJobs until the right opportunity turns up. When a "good" job does come along, however, employee loyalty will be far more positively based than it was in previous decades. Workers who stick with a company will do so because they like their jobs, not because they're afraid of losing them. Salary and a measure of job security will both be important, of course, but job satisfaction will be the key factor in determining whether a worker stays on board or jumps ship. Where company loyalty is concerned, management's job will be to determine *exactly* what the organization needs and what workers want—and then to negotiate terms of employment that will meet those mutual requirements as closely as possible. Organizational loyalty may be more short term in the future, but that will only make it more essential for leaders to understand how to gain the commitment of talented workers—and how to do it quickly. The process for renegotiating the "compact" between employers and employees is covered in Chapter 6. For now, here are a few guidelines to keep in mind:

• Don't assume that employees are indifferent about commitment and loyalty. In a study I conducted with 1,000 employees, 95 percent said that "collecting a paycheck" wasn't all they wanted out of their jobs. They also wanted to work for an organization they could contribute to and care about.

• Let employees know exactly what the organization offers and what it expects of them in return. One of the most important functions of leadership is communicating the linkage between the organization's values, vision, and goals and the changing roles and responsibilities of workers.

• If you want employees to trade in the paternalism of the past, make sure you are offering them a true partnership in return.

• Don't judge employee commitment by old-fashioned standards of behavior. Charlie Lynch, the CEO of Fresh Choice, noted: "Loyalty isn't dead, it's simply manifesting differently. Some old-school managers just haven't figured that out yet." (Hint: Don't expect Gen-Xers to display their commitment to the organization by blindly following orders.)

• "Benchmark" other models of work relationships to discover how television shows, motion picture companies, or football teams bond highly talented professionals to the goals of the enterprise without guaranteeing perpetual employment. Then decide which factors—the opportunity to enhance reputation/visibility within the industry, the chance to affiliate with a winning organization, the development of desired professional skills, and so forth—could also be used to build commitment in your company?

• Move away from a "them" versus "us" workplace mentality by creating a management–employee "Commitment Task Force" to create organizational policies, procedures, and programs that are mutually beneficial.

The Contingent Work Force

One area of relationship friction in the workplace has resulted from the replacement of the large, permanent employee bases that characterized enterprises in the past by new, more adaptable models of organization. The shift is to a focus on in-house core competencies and the contracting out of as many of the other tasks as possible—often to smaller, more specialized companies and even to individuals who can do the work faster, better, and cheaper. Corporations are deliberately hollowing themselves out today, reducing permanent staff to a minimum, and carrying out as many activities as possible at dispersed locations. Charles Handy, at the London Business School, calls these "minimalist, partly unseen organizations" the "linchpins of our world." The three-tier model is one example of a new structure. In this system, a company is organized around three groups of employees: core, conditional, and contract workers. Core employees are a small, relatively permanent "core" of highly adaptable employees whose broad skills allow them to tackle a wide variety of projects in-house. Conditional workers can be added or eliminated quickly, as needed. Contract workers are outside experts whose subcontracted specialties support core competencies.

Although a larger proportion of adults now participate in the U.S. labor force than 30 years ago, increasingly they are subcontractors, part-timers, and temporary workers. In the United States, the number of individuals employed by temporary agencies has increased 240 percent in the past 10 years. Depending on how broadly one defines the term, there are between 2.7 million and 6 million contingent workers in America.

When you consider these figures as they relate to organizational dynamics, they point to the ongoing challenge of melding a work force of full-time, permanent employees with their part-time and contracted counterparts. Transferring work traditionally done by employees to elements of the contingent labor force alters relationships and brings new sources of organizational friction. Temporary employees may have little or no attachment to the company at which they work. Regular employees are dismayed to see temporary workers take the place of laid-off colleagues and often take it as a sign that the organization does not have employee interests at heart. Another source of work force friction comes when specific jobs or entire departments are outsourced, and workers performing the same function are told that they no longer work for the company but for a contractor. (These "newly created" contract employees experience the same sort of psychological shock we see in workers who were part of a merger or acquisition.)

There is no simple solution to this challenge, but a good place to begin is by letting the work force know that you are aware of the situation and then assembling a problem-solving team of permanent, part-time, and temporary employees to explore ways to develop working relationships that support the goals of the entire organization.

Rewards and Entitlements

Financial security is no longer the sole consideration for employees when they choose a job. Expect workers at all levels to want more than just a paycheck in return for their contributions to their companies. Along with such alternative material rewards as profit sharing, productivity bonuses, stock-buying options, and more company perks, workers deciding on a company will also be looking for intangible paybacks ranging from greater control over working circumstances to such in-house services as financial and emotional counseling, fitness clubs, child-care facilities, medical/dental care, and provision for leisure activities. Providing a more congenial and caring workplace environment will cost something—but having continually to hire and retrain new employees costs something too. And research is already showing that money spent on a work force's sense of belonging and well-being is more than paid back by increased effort and commitment to company goals.

On the benefits side, sick-leave and health-care packages are going to climb the priority list as state and federal safety nets are further withdrawn in coming years. Retraining programs and greater access to alternative career paths within a company will be seen as central to the future employee's sense of entitlement. So will work that offers greater intellectual challenge and the chance to exercise more individual initiative. And as social security benefits fall further behind the cost-of-living index, company-managed retirement and pension programs are also going to become steadily more important in the work force's list of demands.

New-Age Issues

Allied to the work force's deepening mistrust of authority is a growing spirit of concern for the effect of exploitative business practices on individual, community, and global well-being. New-age issues, ranging from self-realization to resource pollution are already influencing corporate thinking about medium- and long-term goals. The day when U.S. workers, concerned only with job security, were prepared to see their companies make an extra buck from the destruction of a lake, an endangered specie's habitat, or their own souls has long since passed.

Workers today—and certainly in the future—will only give their best to companies whose ethical visions they approve of and whose management practices encourage positive, responsible contributions that lead to more than just monetary reward. Workers want their work to mean something today; they want to feel valuable in themselves for what they do, and they want to feel that what they do adds value, however minutely, to the quality of their own, their colleagues', and the world's life.

This may sound like new-age mumbo-jumbo. But believe me, it isn't. Ask the blue-collar worker who used to fish his local river on weekends and can't now because the company he works for killed the river dumping toxic waste. Ask the working mother who's had to go on extended sick leave because of work-related stress syndrome. Ask the employee who's had to seek psychiatric help because of management bullying, or the senior vice president who discovered what peace of mind really means in a Buddhist ashram. Ask anybody you like. Concern for the environment, concern for society, concern for the individual, concern for spiritual and emotional well-being, concern for quality over quantity are all back on the agenda. Company managers who fail to take note of that agenda are going to find it more and more difficult to recruit the best people. And without the best, their companies won't survive. According to Robert Haas, the CEO of Levi Strauss & Co., "By sticking with conventional wisdom and conventional practice—and not daring to take the lead in social practices as well as business practices—you're dooming yourself to extinction."

• Indianapolis-based Walker Information recently released the results of a survey measuring the impact of good citizenship on a company's bottom line. The study found that 46 percent of the employees surveyed were involved in employer-sponsored community service projects in the past year, and that those involved were 30 percent more likely to want to continue working for their company and help it be a success.

• Levi Strauss blends outstanding business performance with what a writer at *Fortune* termed "conspicuous decency." When Levi found out that two of its sewing subcontractors in Bangladesh were using child labor, it also discovered that if the children lost their jobs, some of them might be driven into prostitution to survive. The solution that Levi devised was to take the children out of the factory, continue paying their wages on the condition they attend school full-time, and then guarantee them factory jobs on reaching 14, the local age of maturity.

• Community service and volunteerism have long been a part of AT&T's culture. In 1996, the organization extended its commitment to volunteerism through AT&T CARES—the first time a major corporation offered paid community service involvement to its entire work force. Through the AT&T CARES program, in 1996 all 127,000 employees around the world had the opportunity to take one paid workday to perform community service. This was an investment of approximately one million hours of volunteer time, at a cost to the company of $20 million. Feedback from employee volunteers and the agencies they served was extremely positive. "It makes me feel wonderful," said one AT&T employee in Jacksonville. "It's great to have your employer give you a paid day to give something back to your own community."

• Anita Roddick, the CEO of The Body Shop, talks openly about her commitment to the environment and to social issues. She says, "I don't want our success to be measured only by financial yardsticks or by our distribution or number of shops. What I want to be celebrated for—and it's going to be tough in a business environment—is how good we are to our employees and how we benefit the community."

THE GHOST IN THE MACHINE

The term is Arthur Koestler's. "Machine" refers ironically to the human brain; "ghost" names a hypothetical flaw in the brain's evolution that produced a split between reason and emotion as man advanced into the modern age. A similar split exists in too many U.S. businesses today: a temperament division between corporate goals and work force needs that must be bridged if those businesses are going to remain front-line competitors in the new global economy. Changing work force expectations arising from diversifying life-styles and a radical realignment of U.S. social values stand on one side of the divide. Corporate aims, driven by the need for greater efficiency and higher productivity, stand on the other. Neither side is going to advance successfully into the next century if each simply holds its ground, glaring across the chasm at its opponent, shaking its collective fist and insisting on the rightness and necessity of its own position. A compromise needs to be reached; a new paradigm to replace the old industrial-age vision of us-and-them employer–employee relations needs to be drawn up and signed by both sides in a spirit of equal commitment. The ghost in the business machine is intransigence. And the first step in exorcising intransigence is taken when worker and manager alike realize that a business actually isn't a machine at all but a mutually dependent community of human beings.

CHAPTER 2

I Thought We'd Already Found the Right Answer

Second Step: Adopt the New Business Paradigm

We are in one of those great historical periods that occur every 200 to 300 years when people don't understand the world anymore, when the past is not sufficient to explain the future.

Peter Drucker, Professor,
Claremont Graduate Center

In the sixteenth century, the Polish astronomer Nicolaus Copernicus discovered that the earth revolves around the sun. With this simple observation, Copernicus created a heresy and a "revolution." The dethronement of the earth from the center of the universe called for the rethinking of almost every religious and scientific "truth" mankind had relied on for the past 5,000 years. This wasn't just a paradigm shift, it was a paradigm shift on a grand scale.

Paradigms are simply agreed-on models of the way things appear to work. They are, in a sense, the formalized reference points of our belief systems. But, as the Copernican revolution demonstrates, they are not immutable and they are not eternal. Paradigm shifts, as Thomas Kuhn explained in *The Structure of Scientific Revolution,* occur whenever the way we understand the world is so in conflict with our experience of the world that the old model stops serving any useful purpose—when action based on a given model no longer produces the desired or expected results. The business world is experiencing such a paradigm shift today, not because some Harvard economics professor proclaimed a fundamental error in our concept of business dynamics but because business dynamics themselves have evolved beyond the model that gave rise to them 200 years ago. The forces discussed in the first chapter—the shift to a global economy, the impact of new technologies, the power of the consumer, the move from manufacturing to service, and the changes in the character of the work force—have combined to dethrone past truths about organization, leadership, and business strategy. To paraphrase Drucker, "The certainties of the past are no longer sufficient to inform the policies of the future."

The paradigm on which all businesses have structured themselves since the industrial revolution derives from the laws of Newtonian physics. Its defining characteristic is its resemblance to a machine, and its longevity can be explained by the simple fact that up to about 30 years ago it worked. Then, with the end of the industrial age and the advent of the new global economy, it stopped working. Predictions started going awry. Results began falling short of expectations. All kinds of practical problems began surfacing that could not be resolved by referral back to the old mechanical model.

At about the same time, corresponding problems were surfacing in physics. The order and predictability of Newtonian science were beginning to conflict with new discoveries. The universe, it seemed, was not all that orderly after all; chaos, it soon became evident, was an integral part of its makeup. "For the first time in 300 years," Fritjof Capra wrote in *The Turning Point,* "physicists faced a serious challenge to their ability to understand the universe. . . . The new physics necessitated profound changes in concepts of space, time, matter, object,

and cause and effect; and because these concepts are so fundamental to our way of experiencing the world, their transformation came as a great shock."

Today's business leaders are experiencing a similar shock
with the breakdown of the old business paradigm. But whereas
the universe will go on running however physicists react to its
newly discovered dynamics, businesses will not. "Many scientists," Thomas Kuhn wrote, "remain emotionally attached to
theories that have long since been disproved. Ignoring overwhelming evidence, they will go to their graves stubbornly
clinging to their limited but familiar points of view." Unfortu-
nately, business leaders who follow that example are going to
see their companies arrive at the graveyard long before they do.

THE NEW BUSINESS PARADIGM

The problem I deal with most frequently today is the corporate
struggle to energize employees using a model of reality that no
longer matches current workplace experience. If change *is* the
new reality—and believe me, it is—then the only business paradigm that's going to produce positive results today is one that
includes instability as a positive element. Newton's rational,
predictable universe is no longer our universe. Not in science or
in business.

The foundation for both is shifting:

- From predictability to uncertainty
- From linear progression to discontinuous leaps
- From objective to subjective
- From control to boundaries

From Predictability to Uncertainty

In the Newtonian paradigm, all of nature was knowable through
observation and subject to the laws of mathematics. This same

view of reality formed the foundation for management thought in the industrial age. We operated with the conviction that there was always a right answer to be found if we looked long and hard enough. In our educational system we stressed facts and rewarded those who found the one right answer to questions. In business, if we couldn't find perfect solutions when we managed enterprises, we hired consultants who told us that they could. The organization was orderly and stable, and all change was deterministic, following a predetermined and predictable path. Disorder, variation, and instability were viewed as counterproductive. Management's role in the linear, mechanical business paradigm was to create predictability, stability, and control.

The arrival of quantum mechanics changed all that for science. Physicists studying particles at the subatomic level found that there is no stability, no single right answer, and no predictability. Similar circumstances are impinging on the business world today. New technologies, shifting customer preferences, and unexpected government decrees come seemingly from nowhere to change some industries and make others obsolete. As Ken Derr, the chairman of Chevron, says, "In the future, change will not be a force in the environment, it will *be* the environment."

I don't mean to minimize the difficulty people are going to have accepting the fact that uncertainty is normal and to be expected. But I do want to emphasize the fact that difficult or not, uncertainty is the only dependable thing going for you today. My friend Alan Sauer, retired chief executive of the San Jose Board of Realtors, told me that managing in today's world was like working with wet clay: "The good part is that when clay is wet it is at its most pliable stage, which makes it a great time to mold totally new structures and ways of dealing with each other. The difficult part is that the clay never gets to dry— never gets to feel permanent—and this is very hard on people still hooked on the *illusion* of permanence." Ralph Larsen, the chairman and CEO of Johnson & Johnson, explained it like this: "If we can manage a high level of complexity with a tolerance for ambiguity, it would be an important competitive advantage. People don't like complexity and ambiguity. It ruins their digestion. But the world is that way."

And because (like it or not) the world is that way, companies need to share that complex and ambiguous reality with their employees. Leaders who continue to position their current strategy as the "right answer" to the challenges of the future are encouraging employees to anticipate a spurious return to stability as soon as the correct structure/product mix/staffing, and so on is in place. And when this state of permanence doesn't result—when the *next* "right answer" is announced and last year's strategy discarded—employees become more skeptical, more resistant, and less willing to believe that the company leadership has *any* idea of what is going on at all.

In a recent interview for *Fortune* magazine, Larry Bossidy, the CEO of AlliedSignal, said: "I don't think the strategic plan of yesterday has anything to do with the strategic plan you need for tomorrow . . . I want our people to know that what you do in a strategic plan yesterday can be appropriately discarded tomorrow—and with no shame and no blame but rather a recognition that the marketplace has changed and therefore we have to change."

How are you positioning your present corporate strategy—as a permanent solution or as *today's* best plan to meet an unpredictable future?

From Linear Progression to Discontinuous Leaps

Linear relationships are easy to think about. The pieces add up. Nonlinear relationships are harder to grasp because they lack apparent logic. James Gleick uses this example about ice hockey in his book, *Chaos*. "If you eliminate friction, there is a linear amount of energy needed to accelerate the hockey puck. Friction complicates the relationship. The amount of energy changes depending on how fast the puck is already moving. You cannot assign a constant importance to friction because it depends on speed, which depends on friction."

Discontinuity (nonlinear leaps in a transformation process) is intrinsically threatening. People can accept a certain amount of linear, incremental change, but discontinuous change provokes confusion and anxiety. Just as there are human genes with no instructions other than to resist mutation, some human beings seem to come equipped with no other temperamental programming than to resist organizational transformation.

Benoit Mandelbrot's work with discontinuous equations in the 1960s showed the advantage of embracing discontinuity instead of struggling to resist it. He used nonlinear equations (repetitive loops that feed the answer back into the equation thousands upon thousands of times) to graph "fractal" designs. Besides being a more accurate representation of the world than the smoothed-out cones and cylinders of traditional geometry, fractals lead to a positive appreciation of discontinuity as a source of reassurance that what first appears to be senseless irregularity actually has an underlying order. By focusing on discontinuity rather than trying to smooth it out, fractals help us understand formerly incomprehensible complex, chaotic systems like weather, the stock market, and even the level of violence or passivity in a population.

The same approach holds true for business today. We are experiencing discontinuity of epic proportions, altering the very structure of our organizations, compelling businesses to operate in unpredictable new ways, and most of us are not even remotely prepared. Yet, when properly understood and handled, discontinuity holds tremendous potential for creativity and growth. Charles Handy talks about discontinuity as an opportunity for learning: "Ask people . . . to recall two or three of the most important learning experiences in their lives, and they will never tell you of courses taken or degrees obtained, but of brushes with death, of crises encountered, of new and unexpected challenges or confrontations. They will tell you, in other words, of times when continuity ran out on them, when they had no past experience to fall back on, no rules or handbook."

Monsanto's CEO, Robert Shapiro, is betting his organization's future on what an article in *Harvard Business Review* refers to as "a strategic discontinuity" from the traditional corporate strategy of responding to environmental concerns with incremental improvements. The *Harvard Business Review* article goes on to say that Shapiro sees the conundrum facing his company this way: On the one hand, if a business doesn't grow, it will die. And the world economy must grow to keep pace with the needs of population growth. On the other hand, how does a company face the prospect that growing and being profitable could require intolerable abuse of the natural world? The vision that Shapiro is gambling billions to bring to reality is the concept of "sustainable development"—the dual imperative of economic growth and environmental sustainability. At Monsanto, employees form "sustainability teams" around six issues: measuring the ecological efficiency of Monsanto's processes, developing the methodology to account for the full cost (including the environmental costs) of making and using a specific product, designing measurements that businesses can use to determine whether or not they're moving toward sustainability, forecasting future opportunities to meet human needs with new business/products that don't aggravate (and perhaps even repair) ecological damage, researching global water needs, and studying ways Monsanto might develop and deliver technologies to alleviate world hunger. According to Shapiro:

> Multinational corporations like ours have gotten pretty good at figuring out how to operate in places where we can make a living while remaining true to some fundamental rules. As more countries enter the world economy, they are accepting—with greater or lesser enthusiasm—that they are going to

have to play by some rules that are new for them. My guess is that, over time, sustainability is going to be one of those rules.

How is your organization positioning itself to take advantage of the opportunities offered by discontinuity?

From Objective to Subjective

Under the old Newtonian paradigm, the nature of material reality was determined by what could be observed and measured. Objectivity became synonymous with Truth, and what could not be proven objectively was thought of as somehow hiding its "reality" from empirical scrutiny. A reasonable enough attitude when applied to fields like astronomy, or mechanics, or anatomy, but as British astrophysicist John D. Barrow pointed out in his *Theories of Everything,* "We had come to think of linear, predictable, and simple phenomena as being prevalent in Nature because we were biased toward picking them out for study."

Objective observation as the source of all knowledge was first questioned in the nineteenth century through the study of human psychology and then given a real blasting in the twentieth when quantum physicists studying the behavior of subatomic particles began to realize that the very act of observing interferes with that which is being observed. The physical inconsistencies that emerged when the same elementary matter was studied as particles in one experiment and as waves in another are a little difficult to grasp. But there is a story from zoology that makes the point clearly enough: A team of scientists photographing the mating habits of arctic seals at the North Pole discovered to their surprise that instead of simply getting on with it, the seals first dashed about the ice floes, clapping their flippers and bellowing hysterically until they were so exhausted they literally collapsed in each other's arms. Believing they had discovered something amazing about the sex lives of seals, the scientists showed their footage to a famous professor of zoology who, after a moment's thought, said simply: "And what would *you* do if you were in bed with your wife one night and a gang of strange-looking creatures walked in carrying movie cameras and spotlights?"

In our business organizations, we are only just beginning to comprehend what it means to move from a purely objective perspective to one that includes the intangible, subjective aspects of business. For example, "quality" was conceived as an objective, statistical concept—allowing only so many flaws per 1,000 or 1,000,000, and so on. Today, that thinking is being challenged by such people as Charles Hampton Turner, a professor at the London Business School, who says: "There is no escaping the fact that a product or service can be no better, no more sensitive, esthetic or intelligent than are the relationships and communication of those who create the product or provide the service." If we follow Dr. Turner's statement to its obvious conclusion, quality moves from a purely statistical concept to a relationship issue. Rather than watching the numbers, companies should be looking at the basis of the relationships between customers and employees and between employers and employees. If those relationships are based in integrity and respect, quality will naturally follow.

Relationships are also viewed as an important part of what employees get out of their jobs. Sue Swenson, the CEO of Cellular One, says: "You can't lose sight of the fact that people thrive on social interaction. Employees are, first of all, social beings." Horst Schulze, the president of the Ritz-Carlton Hotels, agrees, "Employees come to work for two reasons: First, to do a good job and to contribute to the organization, and second, to be with their coworkers, their friends. And, by the way, these are the same reasons I come to work."

Because the world of science was thought to be a material world, filled with "hard facts" and subject to objective observation and analysis, it ignored the existence of consciousness—of subjective experience, of values. When we extended the concept of duality to our organizations and management, we focused on quantifiable data and observable behavior and excluded or discounted the "nonmeasurable" dimensions of consciousness, emotion, and creativity. The separation of mind from matter has cost organizations their ability to engage and profit from the most potent, if invisible, gifts their employees have to offer. Only recently are organizations beginning to understand that the intangibles—employees' attitudes, intuition, ideas, creativity, energy, and emotional engagement—are exactly what they need most to succeed in the future. Horst Schulze says: "When I speak with people in the different departments throughout the hotel, employees in every function, from dish washing to marketing, have the same desire for the future—to be the best! This is the positive emotion and the kind of enthusiasm with which everyone starts out when a new hotel opens. The most important job of a leader is to keep that emotion and enthusiasm alive."

What is the quality of the relationships in your organization? What are you doing to engage employees' positive emotions and to keep enthusiasm alive?

From Control to Boundaries

Chaos theory studies the relationship between order and disorder—states now viewed as being integral parts of a single whole—so that systems can react with apparent randomness and yet be held in bounds by forces that give them order. A system is defined as chaotic when there is no predictability to its next immediate action. But if the chaotic system is observed over a long enough period, a pattern arises in which certain boundaries are found to exist. The force that determines the shape of the system is called a "strange attractor," and although a system will never behave in exactly the same way twice, it will also never go beyond the pattern set by the strange attractor.

What creates boundaries in a *boundaryless organization?*

What facilitates decision making when rules and regulations are reduced or eliminated? How do you control an organization in tumultuous times?

The answers to these questions call for radical redefinitions, not only of organizations but of the nature of control. Freedom becomes more important than control. Not freedom that is unlimited or irresponsible but freedom within boundaries. By setting larger boundaries for employees, leaders find less for them to control. Leaders who influence us the most in the future will be those who understand that control is not about rules, regulations, and rewards—or the struggle to keep people "in line." When you think of the qualities that leaders need to encourage in their employees—responsibility, creativity, caring, commitment—you can see why coercion or manipulation just doesn't work.

The principle of the strange attractor shows that even the most erratic and complex system activity has an underlying order. Just as the magnetic influence of the attractor draws a chaotic system into a discernible pattern, so do strongly held values influence the judgments and actions of a work force by creating a boundary beyond which behavior will not go. The most influential leaders are those who understand that guiding principles and organizational values play the central role in shaping work force behavior today, not the list of rules and regulations.

I always take the following example of work force empowerment with me whenever I address leadership conferences around the world. It is the one-page *Employee Handbook* that Nordstrom, the Seattle-based upscale retailer, gives its employees. By now, most business leaders are familiar with the handbook, but few of them view the corporate value it embodies as an example of a strange attractor in action:

> Welcome to Nordstrom. We're glad to have you with our company. Our number one goal is to provide outstanding customer service. Set both your personal and professional goals

high. We have great confidence in your ability to achieve them. Nordstrom rules: Rule #1—Use your good judgment in all situations. There will be no additional rules. Please feel free to ask your department manager, store manager or division general manager any question at any time.

Can you think of a more potent prescription for chaos than inviting everyone in an organization to rely solely on good judgment when making decisions? Yet Nordstrom's work force does not disintegrate into thousands of employees "doing their own random thing." Nordstrom's secret lies in stressing its primary corporate value—outstanding customer service—and then liberating employees *in service to* that value.

What is the criterion for decision making in your organization? Is it found in rule books or guiding principles?

ORGANIZATIONS AS LIVING SYSTEMS

Business leaders often speak to me about the need to create more intelligent, thoughtful, flexible, innovative, positively motivated organizations—organizations that can learn and adapt and relate constructively to changing situations and demands. I always tell them the same thing: None of those characteristics can be found in a machine. They can only be found in *living systems.* Modeling a modern business structure on a clock or a car engine doesn't work anymore. What works today is a structural paradigm derived from a living system: a jazz band, or a baseball team, or a coral reef; even a flock of birds.

At a leadership conference for the International Association of Business Communicators, an IABC chapter leader used a living-systems metaphor to compare teamwork in the regional chapters with the behavior of a flock of geese:

- When geese fly in formation, they travel faster than when they fly at random.
- Geese share leadership. When the lead goose tires, he or

she rotates back down the "V," and another flies forward
to become the leader.

- Geese keep company with the fallen. When a sick or weak
  goose drops out of flight formation, at least one other
  goose joins to help and protect.
- Being part of a team, we accomplish more, faster. Support, compassion, and caring (honking from behind is the
  goose way) inspire those on the front lines, helping them
  to keep pace in spite of pressure and fatigue. It is simultaneously a reward, a challenge, and a privilege to be a contributing member of a team.

The Living-Systems Model of Transformation

Dissipative change is the process by which existing forms of
any organization break up and seek entirely new forms and
structures. The living-systems model of transformation brings
new perspectives for business organizations: Businesses are energized by fluctuations, which in turn drive the processes of
change. Organizations flourish at the edge of chaos—unstable
but not out of control. Information from the internal and external environment flows freely through the organization, and employees have access both to it and to one another. The flow of
information drives continuous improvement and innovation.
Periodically, it also challenges and disrupts existing structures
to create new forms of service delivery, levels of productivity,
and quality. Stability does have a shorter life span in this model,
as processes temporarily manifest themselves in structures
while they get ready for the next transformation. Managers facilitate the disorder. Constant experimentation becomes the
norm. From a corporate mind-set of "multiple right answers,"
local solutions are kept at the local level and not elevated to
models for the entire organization. A strong sense of identity
and purpose keeps the work force focused on a collective goal.
People understand that progress is never a straight line. Uncer-

tainties create the unexpected. The process of change is never over. Instead, change is valued as the creative dynamism, the very life of the system.

This is the model that makes sense of employees' actual experience and encompasses a rationale that will remain valid for the future. But the living-systems model does even more than that. At the end of a recent program to an audience of scientists and engineers, I asked for questions and comments. One physicist raised his hand and said, "I like that model a lot."

"Oh, you do?" I answered, assuming he liked it because he was familiar with the theories underlying it. Of course, my assumption was wrong.

"Yes," he said cheerfully. "I like it because it's comforting."

MANAGEMENT INSIGHTS FROM A LIVING-SYSTEMS MODEL

Behaviors of living systems parallel and explain the behavior of a variety of social and human systems: organizations, management decision making, social behavior.

Insights from living systems include the following:

- There is creative potential in instability.
- Organizations thrive at the "edge of chaos."
- Information is the nutrient of the system.
- Organizational stability comes through a sense of identity and collective focus.
- Unintended consequences are to be expected.
- A large-scale reaction can result from a very small change.
- Self-organization changes management's role and relationship with workers.

This section of the chapter examines how these insights are being put to use today in business organizations around the world.

The Value of Instability

The winners of tomorrow will deal proactively with chaos, will look at chaos per se as the source of market advantage, not as a problem to be got around.

Tom Peters, *Thriving on Chaos*

Contrary to the Newtonian mechanical model, a living-systems model welcomes turbulence, uncertainty, and instability as essential to the the creative process of nature. The best opportunities for positive change come not with stability (which ultimately results in stagnation) but with the instability created when new information causes flux within the system and pushes it to seek novel and innovative ways to meet the new challenges created. The basic business response to disruption needs to change from trying to get things back to normal to utilizing the disruption as a stimulus for the exploration of new possibilities.

Clearly, the greatest advantages go to those who anticipate instability, see the opportunities it offers, and embrace them early on. Royal Shell saved billions of dollars in the 1973 and 1979 oil crisis by anticipating the unusual. Shell's planners realized that some OPEC countries were making more money than they needed and that their leaders, knowing oil was a finite resource, feared they would eventually lose their incomes entirely. In contrast, conventional industry wisdom held that oil was cheap and infinitely plentiful and that oil-producing countries were so competitive and so suspicious of each other that they could never work together to restrict output for long. In the conventional view, the idea of jointly raising petroleum prices without one of them eventually undercutting the floor figure was simply unthinkable. Shell, doubting this conventional view, took action based on a much less likely sounding scenario: Oil-producing nations, they predicted, *would* form a cartel, *would* curtail output, *would* raise the price of oil, and *would* stick to their guns. Rather than rest complacently in the unchallenged assumptions of the status quo, Shell's managers were prepared to take an informed strategic risk and look seriously at the potential opportunities offered by the instability they saw approaching. When the OPEC embargo became a reality, only Shell was ready to respond positively. Shell changed its refinery investment and oil field location strategies and altered its forecasts. Rather than "circling the wagons" or becoming more centralized, Shell responded to instability by giving its operating companies more freedom to expand. Shell increased its global market share by 8 percent within two years.

Self-organizing systems are adaptive; they don't just respond to events passively, they actively seek ways to take advantage of them. The human immune system adapts actively to new infections, animals adapt to new habitats and food supply, the human brain constantly organizes and reorganizes its billions of neural connections to learn from new experience, whole species evolve for survival in changing environments. Corporations and industries must learn to do the same thing.

When Lars Kolind, the CEO of Oticon, wanted better products and stronger profits in his hearing aid manufacturing company in Denmark, he used instability as a way to establish an urgency for change. Kolind dissolved the entire formal organizational structure, did away with job titles and descriptions, and formed an in-house interior decoration committee to redesign headquarters with lounge areas, coffee bars, and more open and casual work-floor arrangements. He declared that everyone should have a "multijob"—their area of specialization *and* whatever interested them. He created and focused the organization on the following corporate slogan: "Think the unthinkable." Kolind's efforts at Oticon caused a lot of confusion for employees. Managers were told to re-create their jobs but were not given instructions how to do it. Employees were left alone to sort out which people were best suited for working in this new kind of flexible and dynamic environment. Innovation was encouraged through unstructured gatherings where employees discussed, argued, and debated. Risky? You bet. But at Oticon the risk paid off. Employees developed the new processes and products which soon raised corporate profits.

Thriving on the Edge of Chaos

Jazz—like business—implies a series of balancing acts. It must always be disciplined—but never driven—by formulas, agendas, sheet music. It must always be pushing outward, forward, upward—and therefore, inevitably, against complacency.

                                        John Kao, *Jamming*

It is essentially meaningless to talk about a complex adaptive system being in equilibrium because a system by nature is always unfolding and always in transition. However, a living system *can* manifest turbulence and coherence at the same time. Instability is a critical element in the survival and transformation of all living systems, and yet in business we all know that too much instability can weaken an organization. If existing structures and interactions are to respond to environmental demands, the system must strike a balance between the need for order and the imperative for change. Complex living systems have evolved the ability to bring order and chaos into a special kind of dynamic balance called the "edge of chaos." The edge of chaos for business organizations is developed when there is a balance between the traditional and the new, between order and freedom, between the need to maintain standards and the urge to experiment, and between the value of expertise and the input from fresh perspectives.

Skaltek AB is a Swedish company that designs, manufactures, and sells heavy machinery used by the wire and cable industry. Its custom-built machines—state of the art and computer controlled—are sold in 40 countries around the world. Skaltek is not a traditionally structured organization in any sense: There are no titles, no supervisors, no janitors, no receptionists, no phone operators, no private secretaries, no sales or marketing department, and no quality-control department. Instead, there is a community of peers—"Responsi-bles"—who serve on teams that form and disband as necessary to fill customer orders or perform company projects. Chaotic? It certainly could be. But what keeps the dynamic balance at Skaltek is a corporate culture that includes the importance of each individual developing a personal vision (a sense of purpose in life that is inclusive of, but goes beyond, doing his or her job) and an organizational culture of personal accountability. All Responsibles coordinate their schedules with team members, visit customers, clean up after themselves (the plant is virtually spotless), and, after assembling and testing a module that goes into a machine, affix a personally initialed aluminum label on the assembly which reads, "I'm Responsible." Skaltek's products enjoy a worldwide reputation of high quality, state-of-the-art design, and reliability.

The Power of Information

Knowledge is power . . . if you know it about the right person.

Anonymous

Information lies at the heart of natural life, lodged in the DNA. Life uses that information to organize itself into material form. Nobel prize-winning biologist Gerald Edelman says: "What they have found is truly startling . . . when you are born, you have all the information in your antibody system that you will ever need in your whole life to recognize anything you may encounter, including things that don't exist!"

Information is the fuel of complex adaptive systems. In business, information flowing in and out provides the turbulence, the disequilibrium that pushes the organization to transform. Leaders must be the champions of information access. As one consultant put it, "My most important function is to feed back organizational data to the whole organization. The data is often quite simple, containing a large percentage of information already known to many. But when an organization is willing to give public voice to that information—to listen to different interpretations and to process them together—the information becomes amplified. It grows and feeds on itself, building in significance."

Information has to be welcomed everywhere in the organization to nourish the system. The optimal culture is an information-rich culture that discloses its inner workings to everyone—not just to the upper echelon. In command and control cultures, people guard knowledge as their claim to power. Today's empowered workers need more information about the business. You cannot ask people to exercise broader judgment if their access to pertinent information is restricted. When Öystein Skalleberg founded Skaltek, he intended to involve employees in all aspects of the business. Every Monday all workers attend "Information Cash Flow," a companywide meeting at which they get a full report of the previous week's sales, expenses, and profits. At Skaltek there are no financial secrets. If you interview employees at Skaltek, you'll hear people say, "I find it quite natural to know it all. If you work in the dark, you really don't know what you contribute."

Advances in information technology allow organizations to spread information quickly and efficiently throughout the company. Today, the latest innovation to win the attention of the corporate world is Web technology. The Internet offers businesses new opportunities to reach customers. Lately, however, organizations are taking Web technology and turning it inward to create "intranets." A March 1996 *Business Week* cover story offered the definitive explanation: "By presenting information in the same way to every computer, intranets can do what computer and software makers have frequently promised but never delivered: Pull all the computers, software, and databases that dot the corporate landscape into a single system that enables employees to find information wherever it exists."

Katherine Woodall, director of employee communications at Levi Strauss & Co., gave me her perception:

The first issue we identified when considering the value of an intranet—the ability to capture and share knowledge—was logical enough, but required some justification. Why *would* Levi place such a premium on capturing knowledge and creating a consistent platform of the best thinking across the company—and make a large investment in high technology to do so? Because, while the process of making clothing is easy to grasp and the basic patterns haven't changed much in a long time, the marketplace *has* changed dramatically. In fact, it's constantly changing, always keeping us on our toes. Accordingly, the way we do business must keep pace with the changes happening all around us. Today, Levi Strauss & Company is a global enterprise operating in more than 60 countries. Competition is fierce everywhere we do business. Our success depends largely on continuous innovation and superior customer service. Both are fueled by a steady stream of knowledge throughout the company.

Stabilizing through Identity and Collective Focus

One of the fundamental characteristics common to all living beings without exception is that of being objects endowed with a purpose.

**Nobel Laureate and Biologist,
Jacques Monod**

In an open organization, where flux and instability are embraced as positive, life-enhancing attributes, stability is maintained through corporate identity and collective focus of purpose. The leader's role is to create this stability through a constant reinterpretation of the company's history, present activities, and future aspirations. By doing this, leaders can allow all other activities to be mutable. As the CEO of Coca-Cola, Robert Goizueta, states: "At the end of every year, two things remain unshakable. Our constancy of purpose and our continuous discontent with the immediate present."

Corporate culture derives from a nexus of basic assumptions about how to interact with one another and how to handle challenges that a given group of employees discovered or developed and then spread throughout the organization as a kind of world view. A corporate culture that is clear and consistent, and reflects a constancy of purpose, is a stabilizing force. Identity thus permeates the successful organization and is passed on to generations of workers through corporate legend and lore.

Nordstrom does a remarkable job of using anecdotes about its sales force to communicate a culture of impeccable customer service that is central to its identity. For example, management tells the following story—and there are a lot more like it—to Nordstrom employees as an example of work force "heroism." One saleswoman took her lunch hour to drive from downtown Seattle to the airport to make sure that her customer received his new business suit. The customer had purchased the suit that morning to wear at a meeting in another city the next day—and then discovered that the garment needed alterations. The Nordstrom saleswoman promised to have the suit altered and delivered to him before he left town. She kept her promise.

The success of the storytelling approach is evident with both internal and external audiences: To employees it demonstrates that they can go to almost any length to serve the customer and not only will they be operating in good Nordstrom tradition but their stories may be used as heroic examples for others. To the public, these stories create an awareness of Nordstrom's culture; even those who *don't* work there know the corporation's guiding values and, with rare exceptions, admire them enormously.

Unintended Consequences

I'm not afraid of death. It's just that I don't want to be there when it happens.

Woody Allen

In the natural world, complex adaptive systems include brains, immune systems, ecologies, and ant colonies. In the social world they include political parties and business corporations.

Each of these systems has a network of individual "agents" acting in concert. In a brain the agents are nerve cells; in a corporation the agents might be departments, functions, or individuals. Each agent functions in an environment produced by its interactions with other agents in the system. The relationships between agents are the conduits for the intelligence of the system. The more access people have to one another, the more possibilities arise for creating innovative solutions to challenges faced by the whole system. But within these myriad actions, interactions, and shifting relationships, uncertainties and unintended consequences also exist.

I recently spoke to employees of a utility company in southern California. Because the company wanted the entire work force to attend, I spoke once in the morning and repeated the program in the afternoon. At the first session I had just finished covering the material on uncertainty and unexpected consequences when an audience member asked, "If everything is uncertain, what happens to strategic planning? How can you make any plans for the future?"

It was a good question, and I answered it by using the two sessions as an example:

> I was hired to put on two identical programs today, but you and I both know that it is impossible for them to be identical even though I will use the same set of notes for both presentations. The differences will be determined by the makeup of the two audiences—how many attend, what their energy level is, what questions they ask, maybe even what they had for lunch. And, of course, I too will be slightly different depending on my energy level and what I had for lunch, etc. I don't know *how* the afternoon session will be different, but I'm certain that the unexpected will happen.

What all this means to me as I prepare for programs—and to a company as it prepares for the future through strategic planning—is that we have to make our plans taking into account a multitude of contingencies in a volatile environment. And despite our best efforts, the future may or may not play out the way we anticipated. The trick is not to let the unexpected throw us. It's just part of the game.

The Effect Is Disproportional to the Cause

Change takes infinitesimal differences . . . and blows them up in your face.

James Crutchfield, Physicist

In 1960, meteorologist Edward Lorenz created a computer model that simulated weather patterns. In his book, *Chaos,* James Gleick talks about the inception of this model:

> With his primitive computer, Lorenz had boiled weather down to the barest skeleton. Yet, line by line, the winds and temperatures in Lorenz's printouts seemed to behave in a recognizable earthly way. They matched his cherished intuition about weather, his sense that it repeated itself, displaying familiar patterns over time, pressure rising and falling, the air stream swinging north and south. . . . But the repetitions were never quite exact. There was a pattern, with disturbances. An orderly disorder.

By the 1980s, supercomputers with advanced versions of computer modeling changed the weather business from an art to a science. Nevertheless, beyond two or three days, the world's best forecasts were still speculative, and beyond six or seven days, they remained essentially useless. The "Butterfly Effect" was the reason. Technically called *sensitive dependence on initial conditions,* the Butterfly Effect demonstrates how tiny discrepancies at the beginning of a system's evolution make accurate prediction of its outcome impossible. It is so named because of the hypothesis that the way in which a butterfly flaps its wings in Brazil could eventually cause a hurricane on the East Coast of the United States.

Weather is a dynamically interdependent system in which one extremely small event can provoke a major, systemwide change. In all dynamic systems, inescapable consequences emerge from the way small-scale events intertwine with large ones. A chain of events can have points of leverage that magnify small changes. Complexity means that such points are pervasive. We've intuitively understood this magnification for a long time. "For want of a nail, the kingdom was lost" refers to a sequence of events beginning with a relatively minute one (the lost nail) which resulted in the horse throwing a shoe, which resulted in the rider being bucked off, which resulted in the battle being lost and then eventually the entire kingdom: all because of a missing nail. Likewise, when a tiny "O Ring" cracked, it destroyed the Challenger Space Shuttle, which, in turn, resulted in significant doubts about the entire NASA Shuttle program.

Such disproportionate relationships between cause and effect often defy management's best efforts to predict and control. What looks like a solution today may result in a larger problem tomorrow. You cannot possibly anticipate all the potential leverage points in your organization, but you can stay alert for the first signals of overreaction (by continually getting feedback from customers, supplier, employees, and competitors) so that you can respond rapidly.

The Capacity for Self-Organization

The notion of self-organization in human systems may suggest to some that the manager has no real role. The reality is that management has a different role; rather than controller, the manager becomes a liberator.

L. Douglas Kiel, *Managing Chaos and Complexity in Government*

If complex systems are composed of many independent agents interacting with each other in a great many ways, it is the very richness of these interactions that allow the system as a whole to undergo spontaneous self-organization: Atoms form chemical bonds and become molecules; birds adapt to the behaviors of their neighbors and organize themselves into flocks. Teams transcend themselves to become more than the sum of their individual parts. In every case, it happens without a blueprint or conscious plan. The realm of computer networks is a created world, built on an intentionally organic, anarchy-inspiring skeleton. "Chat groups" form around their special interests, linking people from every conceivable background and demographic segment. Just as there is no master neuron in the brain, no computer in the Internet "web" means more than another. To create a business around a living-systems model is to give an organization the freedom to realize its organic capacity to self-organize without any externally imposed plan or direction. This means that leaders have to believe that the work force has the innate ability to respond to continuous change, to create temporary structures and relationship as required, to experiment, and to find simplified and more effective ways to get results.

Xerox Corporation found the value of self-organization in the 1980s when it was looking for a way to boost the productivity of its field service staff. An anthropologist from the Xerox Palo Alto Research Center traveled with a group of technical representatives to observe how they actually did their jobs—not how they described what they did, or what their managers assumed they did. The anthropologist discovered that the reps spent more time with each other than with customers. They'd gather in common areas like the local parts warehouse or around the coffee pot and swap stories from the field. An old-model company manager would have viewed the time spent socializing as a "gap" to be eliminated for higher productivity, but the anthropologist saw the exact opposite.

For Xerox, the informal gatherings didn't represent time wasted but, rather, money in the bank. For it was here, within these self-organized *communities of practice*, that the reps asked each other questions, identified problems, and shared new solutions as they devised them. And it was through conversations at the warehouse—conversations that weren't part of any formal "business process" or reflected in any official organizational chart—that knowledge transfer took place. Thanks to the anthropologists, Xerox is now experimenting with "elegantly minimal processes" that *under*prescribe formal procedures and create more room for local interpretations and innovations, so that more effective business practices can evolve naturally from the grassroots upward, as they should, rather than being imposed from above.

Fritjof Capra writes: "Self-organizing systems . . . tend to establish their size according to internal principles of organization, independent of environmental influences. This does not mean that living systems are isolated from their environment; on the contrary, they interact with it continually, but this interaction does not determine their organization."

Self-managed teams, encouraged to keep their membership "fluid"—to form, adjust the size and composition of the group, even to decide when to disband—follow these same principles. A 1993 problem-solving exercise divided management staff into several teams and assigned each team to prepare simulated bidding on a government bond auction. Some teams were set up with the same people working together throughout the experiment. In other teams, the membership was fluid; people left or were added as the group deemed necessary. The fluid group of teams produced a higher error rate initially but over time made fewer mistaken decisions. The teams with rigid membership became inhibited by their more limited and structured view of the problem, with the result that fewer alternatives and solutions were produced. The "unstable" teams promoted more divergent outcomes and were more readily adaptive to changing situations.

Self-Organization Changes the Role of Leaders

Inevitably, formal hierarchies become less important as people gain increased access to information and begin naturally to seek leadership from whomever has the necessary knowledge or experience. In a self-organized system where leaders emerge organically from situation to situation, it becomes necessary to develop leadership skills in employees throughout the organization. The National Collegiate Athletic Association created a professional development program for its staff. The Team Academy is based on the idea that true empowerment requires leadership to occur in every position within the organization, and that *everyone* in today's work force must have prepared himself or herself to accept the responsibilities and accountability for leading others.

As organizations subscribe to a living-systems model, the criteria for leadership change. Developing leaders for this self-organized work force is very different from developing managers for a bureaucracy. Karen Hendricks, CEO of Baldwin Piano and Organ Company, says:

> I look for four things in potential leaders: (1) out-of-the-box thinking: Do they look for novel ways to solve problems? (2) alignment. Can they get others to support their ideas? (3) respect. How do they get support from others—must they coerce or can they truly inspire people? (4) calculated risk taking. Are they visionary enough to capitalize on the potential upside and analytical enough to calculate (and protect against) the downside?

Leaders today have to be teachers, facilitators, supporters, coaches, and counselors. Horst Schulze, the president of the Ritz-Carlton Hotels, makes these distinctions between the role of a traditional manager and that of a leader:

> A manager manages processes and equipment. Leaders deal with people. Managers tell people what needs to be done and what the punishment is for not achieving the goal. Then

they must watch and supervise people to be sure the goal is met. Leaders establish an environment in which people want to reach goals and contribute to the success of the organization. They align employees with the vision and values of the organization by explaining the higher purpose and importance of everyone's contribution. Throughout our organization, we need fewer managers and more leaders.

In the business world today, as in nature, change can ruthlessly destroy organisms that aren't adaptive. Not all organizations are surviving in the new, radically altered business environment. If you look at the largest 500 companies in 1985 and compare them to the Fortune 500 today, you'll find that 40 percent have ceased to exist. In the past decade at least 700,000 organizations sought bankruptcy protection, more than 800,000 firms were acquired or merged, and more than 450,000 others simply shut their doors because they couldn't compete anymore.

Adaptive organizations must be staffed by adaptive individuals. In a world where flux is the norm, leaders need a work force with the mind-sets and skills that allow it to cope with the continuous flow of new ideas, products, markets, and perspectives. The next chapter looks at how to spot and develop change-adept employees.

3

I Know I Have to Change, But I Don't Know If I Can

Third Step: Develop a Change-Adept Work Force

I have a background in psychology, and in my private practice during the 1980s I counseled hundreds of people who were having problems adjusting to the effects of downsizing and organizational restructuring. (This situation became so common that I built a reputation by specializing in helping individuals deal with change.) When I began giving speeches and seminars to organizations, much of my preparation centered on research into what distinguishes the kinds of people who deal successfully with change from those who don't, or can't, adapt. During the ensuing 12 years, I've spoken on this topic to client organizations in 16 countries around the world—and my research files are still growing.

Just as some organizations cannot survive in a continuously changing environment, some individuals find themselves emotionally overwhelmed when faced with the need to constantly refocus on new tasks and situations. These workers are the victims of change who misdirect their energy by railing against things they cannot hope to influence and fixating on the negative aspects of an uncertain future. They lose heart and look for places to lay blame while abdicating personal responsibility. Longing for stability and certainty, they embody what I call a "Whitman Sampler" mentality. (The Whitman company prints a guide to the candy on the inside of its Sampler box cover.) If Forest Gump's mother was right, and life is like a box of chocolates, these are the people who want a map to the chocolates— and they want the map to be right!

At the opposite end of the spectrum are people whom I label "change adept." These individuals deal with change exceptionally well and are naturally happier in their work because they have come to terms with a world that never stays the same. They move with today's chaotic workplace rather than fighting against it. They are energized by and actually thrive on change.

The change adept are not necessarily more competent than their coworkers, but they have distinct advantages in the attitudes they hold and the strategies they adopt. Change-adept professionals build greater resilience and not only survive but flourish in changing times.

If leaders are going to take a work force successfully into a future of unknowns, the value of having change-adept employees cannot be overstated. This chapter tells how to spot the change-adept professionals in your organization and how to utilize leadership strategies that encourages change-adeptness in the entire work force.

PROFILE OF CHANGE-ADEPT PROFESSIONALS

Basically, five factors determine which people deal successfully with change: confidence, challenge, coping, counterbalance, and creativity.

Confidence

The personality trait most responsible for an individual's ability to deal well with change is self-confidence. Confident people are self-motivated, have high self-esteem, and are willing to take risks. Quite simply, they know how good they are.

In the workplace, self-confident employees are often those who feel secure in the portability of their skills, whose professional networks are intact, and who know they will survive professionally, even if it means finding a new position or a new employer. They recognize their value to the organization and have a realistic perception of their worth in the marketplace. Because they focus on their strengths and strive to develop their talents, they have an obvious advantage over those who may be equally talented but fixate on their limitations and are paralyzed by setbacks. But even the most confident of employees may suffer a crisis of self-doubt in times of change, and it is here that leadership awareness and assistance become critical strategy issues.

Leadership Strategy: Play to People's Strengths

Competence, strangely enough, bears little relationship to confidence. The fact that people on your staff do their jobs very well does not, by itself, ensure that they are also confident of their abilities. It is only when people are *aware* of their competence that they are confident.

Lee Strasberg, the famous acting coach, said, "I can train you in anything except that for which you have no talent." Everyone has areas of lesser and greater talents, and although it can be helpful to acknowledge weaknesses and seek guidance or training to develop those areas, there is nothing more frustrating than striving vainly to excel in areas of endeavor in which one has little or no natural ability.

Talents overlooked may atrophy, and weaknesses—regardless of how much effort is put into trying to improve them—will never match a person's natural strengths. Management expert

Peter Drucker advises, "Don't focus on building up your weaknesses. Understand your strengths and place yourself in positions where those strengths can best be employed. Your strengths will carry you through to success."

We know intuitively that Drucker's advice is sound, but leaders seldom follow it in the workplace. Instead, most workers report that they are singled out for notice only when there is a problem with their performance. Here is a question I often ask my audiences: "If your boss told you that she noticed something about your performance and wanted you to come to her office to discuss it, would you assume that she had noticed an area of your special competence and wanted to bring it to your attention?" Among the majority of audience members who respond with nervous laughter, only a few raise their hand.

Bosses tend to notice and comment on weaknesses and mistakes more than they comment on talents and strengths. Bosses feel it is their role to criticize because the old model for employee improvement is based on what one middle manager refers to as the "If-I-don't-say-anything, you're-supposed-to-know-you're-doing-fine. I'll-let-you-know-if-you-screw-up." mentality. Although continuous learning and self-improvement are valid concepts for future success, focusing solely on what is lacking leads to an unbalanced evaluation of employees' worth and potential. It is no wonder, then, that most workers have problems taking risks and confronting uncertain situations. The focus is on weakness, not competence, and without an awareness or confirmation of their strengths, workers lack the confidence required to embrace change.

Focusing on employees strengths takes a management strategy that includes the following:

- **Don't assume people know how good they are.** I gave a speech for the top management team of a software company in Northern California that was relocating out of state. A few days later the president of the company telephoned me to say,

"After your presentation last week, I began thinking. I have an administrative assistant who is probably the brightest, most creative person I've worked with. The problem is, she's married and can't move her family out of the Bay Area. I was wondering if you would see her for a private counseling session, so that when she applies for a new job, she will come across just as terrific as she really is. I'll even pay for the session."

Of course, I agreed, and looked forward to meeting this talented woman. When she came into my office I said, "This is a real pleasure. I've heard so many nice things about you. Tell me about yourself. What is it that you do exceptionally well? What would you most want a prospective employer to know about you?" The woman was silent for several seconds. Finally she sighed and said, "I really don't know. I do a lot of things well, but when I do them, I don't notice."

• **Notice when employees do something *very* well, and acknowledge it immediately.** Timing is everything when it comes to building talent and strengths. Get in the habit of commenting on outstanding employee behavior as soon as you notice it. When managers at El Torito Restaurants in Irvine, California, catch a worker doing something exceptional, they immediately give the employee a "Star Buck." Each restaurant has a monthly drawing from the pool of stars for prizes (cash, TV, etc.), and each region has a drawing for $1,000 cash.

• **Encourage employees to recognize their own achievements and then "go public."** One manager I know came up with a creative solution to her employees' lament that although she did a pretty good job overall, there were many times when she seemed too preoccupied to notice accomplishments. She put a hand-painted sign in her office and jokingly encouraged employees to display it whenever they had a significant achievement. What started out as an office gag is now a favorite employee ritual. The sign reads, "I just did something wonderful. Ask me about it!"

• **Help employees identify strengths and then find ways to capitalize on them.** Everyone has unique talents and abilities that they do not always use in their present jobs. Todd Mansfield, the executive vice president of Disney Development Company, found that his company was spending too much time on employee weaknesses: "When we'd sit down to evaluate associates, we'd spend 20 percent of our time talking about the things they did well, and 80 percent on what needed to be improved. That is just not effective. We ought to spend time and energy helping people determine what they are gifted at doing and get their responsibilities aligned with those capabilities."

When Paula Banks, the president of Amoco Foundation, worked as human resources director at Sears, she had a secretary who was doing an adequate but mediocre job. Paula talked to the woman and found out that, in her spare time, she was a top salesperson for Mary Kay Cosmetics. In Paula's words: "I found out she had great sales skills, so I changed her duties to include more of what she was really good at—organizing, follow-through, and closing deals. She had this tremendous ability. My job was to figure out how to use it."

• **Set "stretch" goals that pull employees beyond previous levels of achievement.** A former director of recruitment for the United States Coast Guard said that the branch of the service best known for building confidence in its members is the Marine Corps. In his opinion, the reason is that boot camp training constantly challenges Marine recruits to perform beyond their previous physical limits. As a result, recruits take tremendous pride in passing tests of rigorous standards and being found capable.

Most managers I spoke to agreed: "The more you challenge people, the more they'll 'pull up' for it. And when they do—when they actually accomplish the 'impossible'—they begin to realize they are capable of achieving more than they'd ever thought."

• **Create small victories.** To encourage people on the way to achieving goals of exceptional performance, managers need to design "small wins." One executive put it this way, "A stretch goal can scare people to death. I always begin with a mini-goal that I know my staff can achieve, and then I use that victory as a confidence builder for reaching the larger objective."

• **Give *all* employees the opportunity to discover their abilities.** The Office Support Network (OSN) is an inner-company organization of office and clerical workers at S.C. Johnson Wax. Reporting to the head of human resources, it has a 10-member steering committee and 9 subcommittees that address the growth and development of office staff. The chairwoman of the OSN steering committee (also a library clerk) hired me to address its members at their annual dinner meeting and made all the financial and travel arrangements for my engagement. Her experience with the OSN greatly enhanced her opinion of her abilities: "This program has given me a whole new view of myself. I now know that I can conduct meetings and give speeches. For the first time, I feel that I'm a true professional with a lot to offer."

• **At every level of the organization, address weakness but focus on strengths.** It isn't just midlevel managers and front-line employees who benefit from having their strengths reinforced. Ivan Seidenberg, president and chief operating officer (COO) of Nynex, talks about what he values in his relationship with Bill Ferguson, the chairman and CEO: "Bill acts as my coach. He tells me what I need to improve, but he focuses on what I'm doing right. Like everyone else, I need to know what I'm doing right in order to have confidence, take risks, and know that my ideas are of value."

Leadership Strategy: Reward Failure

Some individuals and enterprises would rather run from uncertainty, but they cannot. In a chaotic world, many of the best routes to success require great risks.

Companies attempt radical work reform, which can boost productivity and cut costs but have a high failure rate: They pursue cutting-edge technological innovations that may or may not take hold; they invest in deregulated industries which offer potentially good profits, but with the certainty of intense competition; and they expand into fast-growing developing countries that offer the most lucrative opportunities coupled with the greatest risks.

Individuals who would prefer security are betting on jobs in high-technology industries that offer top salaries today and the serious risk of being swallowed up by the competition tomorrow. Employees who invest their retirement money in hot stocks do so hoping for high returns but face the chance of losing everything.

Change requires gambling and risk, and with risk comes failure. Tom Watson Sr., the founder of IBM, was often quoted as saying, "The way to accelerate your rate of success is to double your failure rate." Bob Metcalfe, president of 3COM, says, "We tell our folks to make at least 10 mistakes a day. If they're not making 10 mistakes a day, they're not trying hard enough."

When people make mistakes or fail in their attempts, self-doubt can become overwhelming. That's human nature. It isn't that change adept professionals are never afraid or doubtful, it is just that they don't let their fears stop them from taking action. Part of their resilience is a philosophy that views failure in a unique way. The change-adept impressed me with their refusal to consider mistakes as defeats. A typical point of view was: "The word *failure* is not in my vocabulary. When I make a mistake, it is just a breakdown showing me exactly what needs to be looked at before I continue along the path—but I am always on the path."

"Failure is not a crime. Failure to *learn* from failure is," said Walter Wriston, the former chairman of CitiCorp. Leaders can begin to develop a work force of confident risk takers by encouraging and even rewarding failure.

One way to encourage risk taking in others is to use your personal failures as examples. Talk openly and honestly about your errors and setbacks—and what you learned as a result. Let people know that you took risks when you were afraid and unsure of the results.

The general manager of an insurance company, concerned that her salespeople were so afraid of failure that they hesitated to take even well-calculated risks, took action at a sales meeting. She put two $100 bills on the table and related her most recent failure, along with the lesson she had learned from it, then she challenged anyone else at the meeting to relate a bigger failure and "win" the $200. When no one spoke up, she scooped up the money and said that she would repeat her offer at each monthly sales meeting. From the second month on, the manager never again got to keep the $200, and as people began to discuss their failures, the sales department became more successful, quadrupling its earnings in one year.

DuPont's Textile Fibers Division actually rewards failure with with a quarterly failure trophy. The failed efforts must have been ethically sound, recognized as failures quickly, and learned from thoroughly.

Leadership Strategy: Build an "Unlearning Organization"

Employees can become psychologically attached to the status quo because it is familiar and comfortable. But even more difficult than fighting off the inertia of comfort, people find it hard to let go of the past because it is there that they experienced personal success—and most people are addicted to feeling competent. Almost everyone likes the experience of mastery— of knowing he or she is doing a good job. That's understandable, that's basic human psychology—it's just not an attitude that helps companies move forward. Although it might have been a valid assumption in the past, when companies valued employees for their entrenched knowledge, the reality of a high-speed future is that current knowledge quickly becomes outdated. In the future, employees will be valued *less* for what they know and more for how quickly they can *learn.* In fact, leaders tell me that one of the greatest challenges of a learning organization is to help employees identify those practices they need to *unlearn* to more quickly adopt new behaviors. Leaders must help employees use past competencies, not as a reason to *stop* learning but as a springboard to future success.

Business leaders help employees to unlearn by addressing the issue directly. They talk about their own problems with unlearning, they empathize with the feelings of awkwardness that people have when leaving their "comfort zone," and they massage damaged egos by applauding the efforts that are being made.

Building a style of corporate behavior that is comfortable with—even aggressive about—new ideas, risk, change, and failure means that workers need to change their attitudes about incompetence. Unlearning, and doing it quickly, is the key to rapid advancement. Instead of labeling incompetence as something to avoid, it should be embraced for what it really is: a positive sign of unlearning. Here are a few questions about learning and unlearning that all employees should be asked to consider:

- What do I do best? (What skills and abilities am I most proud of?)
- How does feeling competent stop me from doing things differently? (Where are the "comfort zones" that I'm most reluctant to leave?)
- What do I need to unlearn? (Which skills are becoming obsolete? What practices—attitudes, behaviors, work routines, etc.—that worked for me in the past are no longer valid?)

- What new skills do I need to learn to stay valuable to the organization?
- What have I learned in the past six months?
- What do I expect to learn in the next six months?

Leadership Strategy: Build Employees' Work Security

Marketplace realities dictate that employees become their own career managers—assessing their strengths and weaknesses, developing personal goals, benchmarking proficiencies, tracking industry and market trends, planning for retirement, and building a portfolio of skills that are transferable to other work situations. As people build "career resilience," they develop an inner security that provides the resources to take care of themselves, even if the company doesn't or can't.

In developing career resilience, employees need the assurance that they'll be told the criteria for success in the future—that the skills and attitudes they need will be clearly communicated—and that assistance in preparing will be available. Leaders endeavoring to foster career resilience have come up with a variety of constructive programs in response.

USS-POSCO, a joint venture with South Korea and U.S. Steel located in northern California, has a learning center that offers a free night school to all employees. Some of the courses are directly job related; others, such as stress-reduction and preretirement planning, help employees take control of their future.

The Regional Municipality of Ottawa offers employees the opportunity to try out short-term assignments in areas of interest at levels higher than the ones they presently occupy, or perhaps even in totally different fields where they can explore and apply transferable skills. The Development Assignment for Regional Employees (DARE) program allows employees to work for a period of up to six months in other parts of the organization at their same salaries and without fear of penalty if failure occurs.

Intel Corporate Staffing is a strategic redeployment process that allows talented employees to move quickly from one business within the organization to another. Intel informs employees about which businesses are declining and which are emerging, so that employees have adequate time and information to plan for their redeployment. Intel utilizes information systems to provide employees with direct input about access to job opportunities and skill requirements and offers resources to assess their existing competencies, identify gaps, hone skills, deepen knowledge, or even retrain completely.

Leadership Strategy: Give Employees "Exit Power"

A few years ago, I spoke at a convention for the American Society of Association Executives in Dallas, Texas. I arrived early to see how the meeting room was set up and to observe the audience reaction as they listened to the speaker on the program ahead of me. I don't recall the speaker's name, but I remember his closing comments:

> My topic this afternoon has been *power,* and I've spoken about several kinds of power, including "positional power," which has to do with your title and level in the organization, and "information power," which comes from your knowledge or access to information. However, there is one kind of power I haven't addressed yet, and without it you will never enjoy any other kind of power in your organization. It is "exit power." If you haven't thought through and developed a plan of action for what you would do if you were fired—written an up-to-date draft of your resume, developed a solid network of business contacts, saved enough money to survive unemployment for several months—then you don't have exit power.

Leaders build work force confidence and loyalty by helping employees develop exit power. I consulted for an oil company at the beginning of its reengineering effort, and during a meeting with the change task force, we began to discuss the drop in confidence the work force was experiencing. One of the managers shook her head. "Not my staff," she said. "Everyone in my department is doing just fine." When we asked her why they were doing so well, the manager said that every week she brought her team together and spent an hour or more going over strategy for various organizational contingencies:

> We look at the current changes going on in the business and the changes we anticipate in the future, and then we plan how best to position ourselves for all outcomes. We plan our personal, financial, and career strategies; we share information and leads about open positions throughout the company; we've even planned a response if our entire function is eliminated. We've decided to stay intact as a department and to sell our services back to the organization.

One leader I know took a novel approach to building employee confidence during a time of organizational upheaval. As a senior vice president of a national bank during a takeover bid by another bank, Norm's department was more productive and his employee retention rate higher than that of other departments. Norm said to me: "I know how unnerving it is not to know what will happen in the future. I understand how confidence levels drop under these conditions. One thing that works for me personally is to give my resume to corporate headhunting firms. It's not that I'm looking to change companies, it's just that I need the confidence that comes only with knowing how desirable I am in the marketplace." He continued, "You know what else I've done? I've told all my managers to circulate their resumes as well."

Challenge

In Chinese, the ideogram for *crisis* combines two characters: One is the symbol for danger, the other for opportunity. The same dual aspects can be ascribed to change. With any change, the danger of possible reversals coexists with incredible opportunities for personal and professional success. Leaders need employees to be excited by the opportunities in change. According to Karen Hendricks, the CEO of Baldwin Piano and Organ Company, "Trying something new and changing the way work is done takes a willingness on the part of employees to take risks and to leave the status quo. What helps me most when I am trying to do a turnaround of a company is knowing there are employees who will take those risks and enthusiastically follow the vision."

When change-adept people are asked for verbal images they associate with change, they acknowledge the stress, uncertainty, pressure, and disruption, but they also emphasize the benefits—the opportunity, growth, adventure, excitement, and challenge.

Long before Dale Carnegie, the human potential movement, or self-help cassettes appeared, experts recognized a positive outlook to be a crucial part of high-level achievement. Cynicism is rampant in organizations, but it occupies little space in the outlook of change-adept individuals. In a fast-moving, high-stress business environment, a positive, upbeat, "can-do" attitude is vital for success.

Although the change adept do not dwell on negativity, they are not oblivious to potential danger. Rather, they analyze situations for both positive and negative aspects, develop strategies to minimize negatives and optimize positives, and then focus on the upside of the situation. Change-adept individuals realize that spending too much time worrying about troublesome aspects or negative outcomes is a waste of mental energy that saps enthusiasm and makes it more difficult to realize the potential opportunities that are also inherent in the situation.

People in an organization who assimilate to change and seek to become involved in it tend to have a much higher self-image when that wave of change passes. Those who are swept along, either unwilling or unable to contribute to the change, are left feeling unsatisfied and disappointed in the way change controlled them. People cannot control all that happens to them at work, but everyone can control how they *respond* to what happens. When will the business stabilize? It won't. Change is with us and will be be with us for the rest of our working lives. No one can escape that fact.

So where does that leave us? I think it leaves us in a similar situation to that in which Winston Churchill found himself when he visited Canada. At a cocktail party, Churchill stood next to a bishop of the church when a lovely young woman passed out glasses of sherry. Churchill took a glass and then the woman offered a drink to the bishop, who refused by saying, "I would rather commit adultery than have a drop of liquor touch my lips." At which point Churchill replied, "Ask the young lady to return. I didn't know we had a choice."

Change-adept people know they have a choice. If change is indeed a fact of life, it is just a fact. And facts are external, objective events over which they may have little or no influence. But reaction, attitudes, and the positive or negative labels they give the facts are all factors over which the change-adept exert choice and control.

Leadership Strategy: Accentuate the Positive

Change is difficult for the people going through it. Change challenges deeply held assumptions and beliefs about careers, personal talents, and the organization's future. It's no wonder that even talented, intelligent employees face change with some misgivings and negativity. A critical element in developing a change-adept work force is knowing how to encourage optimism throughout the work force.

Dr. Henry Goddard, when he was the psychologist at Vineland Training School in New Jersey, measured fatigue in children after criticism and after praise. When they were praised, the children experienced an immediate upsurge of new energy that increased their performance. When they were criticized, the children's energy plummeted.

Further studies on motivation with adults found that telling a group of people they did poorly on solving 10 puzzles decreased their performance on a second try. Telling the group it did well—regardless of whether the praise was deserved—improved performance on a second try.

Criticism is rarely constructive, and praise is almost always energizing and motivating. If you want to develop optimistic employees, praise and thank them. Let people know how much you honor and appreciate their contributions to the organization. Even if those contributions are negligible, nothing is gained—and much may be lost—by criticizing employees you plan to retain in your work force. If criticism is called for, make it positive!

Leadership Strategy: Give Good People the Bad News

Because leaders perceive today's work force to be more cynical and less optimistic than that of a decade ago, they often make a big mistake in their communications. They tend to present factual information about the organization with a too positive "spin," commenting on only the most positive aspects to wary employees. Not only is this misguided communication strategy out of step with the reality that employees experience, it further widens the trust gap between leaders and workers ("Are these executives working in the same company that we are?").

Most important, a diet of all good news does not motivate employees to be more positive and upbeat. Instead of helping develop optimism, the lack of full disclosure actually encourages the rumor mill to fill in the missing communication, often by inventing or distorting information in ways that exacerbate work force apprehension.

A much more effective communication strategy is to level with employees about the current problems and challenges the company is facing so they will have a complete picture of the situation. I was speaking at a meeting sponsored by The Conference Board, and sitting on the same panel of experts was the head of corporate communications from Weyerhauser Corporation. He said that the local newspaper had printed a negative story about the company and its environmental policies. After meeting with senior management, it was decided to rerun the news story in the in-house magazine and next to the negative article to print the company's point of view. The result was that employees were treated as adults and not sheltered like children. They were given both sides of the story and trusted to draw their own conclusions.

Coping

In an environment of constant flux, intellectual capital steadily depreciates. I speak to this issue in my programs when I tell audiences:

> What you know about your industry is worth less right now than when I started this speech. Customer needs have changed, technological progress has raced ahead, and competitors have advanced their plans. Now and for the future, your value to the company increasingly depends less on what you know, and more on how quickly you can learn and how flexible you are in responding to changing conditions.

Some people are naturally more flexible and better at coping with and adapting to a complex, fast-paced reality than others. These individuals take charge of change by accepting responsibility and assuming control. A few years ago, I spoke at a management meeting in Canada for the Saskatchewan Government Insurance Company. At the break, an audience member approached me and said, "What I liked best about your speech was the part about the importance of personal flexibility to deal with change. That's because my father was the head of the Canadian prison system, and he developed a test that was the mark of the criminal mind. Would you like to hear about it?"

I said that I was very interested, so he continued:

> It was really simple. My father would bring each prisoner into his office and sit across from him at a table that had two colored lights—a red one and a green one. My father operated the lights from switches that were hidden under the table. The prisoners' task was simple: When the red light flashed, they were to touch the red light, and when the green light went on, they were to touch the green. All the prisoners could do that just fine, but what none of them could do—so predictably that my father referred to the trait as "the mark of the criminal mind"—was to see the red light flash and begin to move their hands in that direction, and then see the green light go on and alter course in time to touch the green light.

The man waited for my reaction. "You see?" he said. "No flexibility. They couldn't commit to one action and then change course when appropriate. But of course, these were the criminals who'd been caught—the ones who couldn't deviate from set plans even when things weren't working out."

Even a strong corporate culture can prove to be counterproductive if the emphasis is only on stability. A culture that does not encompass organizational fluidity can "lock in" and inhibit change, making the system dangerously vulnerable. A critical element in the health of any organism is robustness: the ability of a system to absorb small jolts. To create a robust organization, you must build flexibility and resilience into its foundation.

An audience member once asked me about the nature of Nordstrom's culture: "What if, in the future, customers don't want all that attention—what if low pricing becomes the most important issue? Would its service culture then become the source of Nordstrom's demise?"

My answer to that is, I don't know. But my hunch is that Nordstrom's corporate value of pleasing customers is resilient enough to shift from the idea of service as we think of it today to "the service of providing the lowest cost," if that is what future shoppers want most.

To be successful in chaotic times, the trick is not to brace yourself for change but to loosen up and learn how to roll with it. In your organization, strategies will be planned, announced, implemented, and then—right in the middle of execution— they will all too often have to be altered or aborted because of external changes. What leaders need from employees is the ability to commit to a course of action and, *at the same time,* to stay flexible enough to alter behavior and attitude quickly to support a new direction. In the big world of life, it's called coping.

Leadership Strategy: Provide Organizational Stress Control

The pressures of business require the ability to manipulate daily stress levels. Although some people burn out under pressure, others use stress to get energized. To them, stress lends zest to life. "Eustress" is the term coined to label a positive level of stress which heightens productivity, creativity, and enjoyment of life.

The mechanism that allows our bodies to handle emergencies is known as the flight-or-fight response. As danger is perceived, the brain stimulates the kidneys to release two sets of hormones. Glucocorticoids increase the level of fats, cholesterol, cortisone, and sugar in the system, and these increase available energy levels to fight or flee a dangerous situation. The second, adrenaline, increases heart rate and, consequently, the body's oxygen consumption.

As this psychophysiological process continues, blood pressure rises and breathing becomes rapid and shallow. Blood is pumped to large muscles and away from smaller vessels; muscle tension increases, as does perspiration needed to cool the active body. Pupils dilate and the senses of hearing and smell become more acute. Brain waves elevate as attention and alertness increase.

When the danger passes, the parasympathetic nervous system reverses the bodily effects to regain equilibrium—homeostasis. As long as we only experience episodic stress—those situations that are comprehensible, specific, and infrequent—we can rely on our bodies to discharge physical tension and automatically rebound in this manner.

You may have noticed this process working for you. If you have ever narrowly avoided an automobile accident, you probably pulled safely to the side of the road with your heart racing and your muscles still tensed for anticipated action. Then, assured that you escaped unharmed, you took a deep breath and began to release built-up tension as your body regulated its functions back to normal.

Stress is basically a response, a flow of energy if you will. A certain amount of stress is necessary for top performance. The only truly stress-free people are dead. Up to a point, stress increases motivation and productivity. When the stress level continues to rise above that point, however, it becomes *dis*tress and negative consequences begin to take effect. Ill effects of negative stress include high blood pressure, headaches, chronic muscle tension, and the general weakening of the immune system. Change-adept achievers have learned how to manipulate stress levels—to generate the right amount of eustress, which for them ensures optimal performance—and to utilize stress-

reduction techniques when they begin to go into stress over-
load.

Distress is the chronic, unabated triggering of the stress response without intervening discharge. Bad stress can also be
triggered by feelings that one's decisions are useless, that life is
out of control. In fact, research shows that the most detrimental work situation is one in which high stress—increased work-
load—combines with low control over how and at what rate the
work is accomplished.

A simple stress-control technique that organizations can implement emphasizes the importance of giving employees autonomy over their work breaks. Studies at California State
University and elsewhere show that employees who are encouraged to take voluntary breaks from tough assignments will outperform those who are denied that freedom. The form of the
break is not important. Some employees close their eyes and
take deep breaths, some get a cup of coffee, others take a walk
or do crossword puzzles. The pertinent factor is that employees
are in control of the timing of their schedule and the content of
their breaks.

Small gestures that show management's concern for workers
can contribute to a more relaxing and less stressful workplace:
At North American Tool and Die, every payday the owners buy
donuts for the entire plant. And during tax season, an accounting firm in San Francisco hired a professional masseuse to give
neck massages to all employees.

Following are a few of the more elaborate strategies used by
corporations to help employees reduce stress:

• **Activities after business hours.** S.C. Johnson Wax
hired a "manager of quality of life," whose job description was
"to find fun and relaxing things for employees and their families
to do after work."

• **Help with personal errands.** At Andersen Consulting
in Chicago, workers typically pay $5 an hour for someone to

pick up dry cleaning, repair shoes, tune up cars, and deliver meals to the office.

• **Recreational facilities.** One of the benefits of working at USAA, an insurance company selling only to current and former military officers, is the 286-acre corporate headquarters near San Antonio, Texas. Within the complex are two walk-in medical clinics with a staff of a dozen nurses, two fitness centers, a five-mile walking/jogging trail and *parcour,* a golf driving range, a softball field, two outdoor basketball courts, and six tennis courts. There are also a number of picnic pavilions, a children's playground, and a fishing lake for use by employee groups or their families on weekends or evenings.

• **Ergonomically designed workplace.** IBM redesigned factory carts to prevent back strain, supplied workers with rubber hand tools to prevent wrist cramps, and redesigned video display terminals to reduce glare and eyestrain.

Leadership Strategy: Don't Make Everything a Crisis

Dean Tjosvold, professor of organizational behavior at Simon Fraser University's School of Business Administration, found that problem solvers worked most constructively when confronted with serious but not critical issues. At moderate stress levels, he discovered, people are more apt to weigh alternatives, solicit opposing points of view, and invite constructive controversy in the problem-solving process.

When faced with a full-blown crisis, however, even experienced professionals can slip, grasp for quick-fix solutions, or take the path of least resistance—anything to bring an end to the emotional turmoil of high stress levels. Similarly, people dealing with problems they perceive as minor do not put forth their best efforts. Under low-stress conditions, the temptation is to ignore the problem or apply pat solutions. What is clear, according to Tjosvold, is that too much stress or too little stress can stymie effective decision making whereas moderate amounts of stress can actually facilitate it.

Some leaders wrongly believe that a "crisis mentality" is necessary to keep a work force from becoming complacent, so they constantly refer to any current situation as disastrous. Keeping a work force in a state of constant crisis is difficult to justify as an effective management strategy: Either employees stop believing that things are as bad as they're being presented (thereby making the organization more vulnerable to a genuine crisis) or they push themselves to respond in a high-stress mode and the organization suffers from employee burnout and inadequate problem solving.

American Airlines CEO Robert Crandall dealt badly with this issue when negotiating a new contract with the pilots' union. During negotiations he used a cover-story interview with the *New York Times* to threaten that if labor costs didn't come down, he faced a crisis that would force him to take his company out of passenger service altogether, sell all his jets, and concentrate on Sabre and other businesses. The pilots responded with less than total belief: "He's cried wolf so many times before that you don't want to hear it anymore," said Captain Jeff Jones, in a *Fortune* magazine article. "We call it 180-degree coding: If Crandall says things are bad, that must mean they are good. Now he tells us that we'll never make it in our business, but we know that the airline earned more than $1 billion in profits last year."

On the other hand, leaders who give employees a well-rounded picture of industry trends, competitive pressures, and customer demands help workers approach business challenges with a realistic idea of the amount of stress needed to do the best job. Don't use crisis as a motivating tactic. It's counterproductive. Be honest. Keep communication channels open and trust employees to respond appropriately to difficult situations. When a real crisis does strike, they'll come through for you—*if* they've been treated responsibly.

Leadership Strategy: Lighten Up

My father-in-law is a vigorous 94-year-old who lives by himself in an apartment in San Francisco. He exemplifies one of the most effective of all change-adept strategies for coping with tough situations—he can laugh at himself. His sense of humor has helped him through many rough spots in life, the latest of which is the loss of his short-term memory. Like many people his age, my father-in-law can tell you in great detail what he was doing in 1924, but he has no idea where he left the portable radio he was listening to this morning. Even with a change as negative as memory loss, my father-in-law uses humor to cope. Here is a story he told me the other day:

> A man and a woman meet in the hallway of their retirement home. They greet each other by name, and then the woman says to the man, "Joe, I bet I can guess your age." Joe replies, "Okay, Sally, how old am I?" Sally says, "First you have to take off all your clothes." Joe looks shocked, but goes along with the strange request and gets completely naked. Sally walks around Joe for several minutes, and finally says, "You are 87 years old." "That's absolutely right," says an amazed Joe. "How did you know?" Sally grins and replies, "You told me yesterday."

A sense of humor and fun are requisites for a change-adept workplace. Leaders should encourage others to lighten up. As the president of a title insurance company said to me, "To survive in this business, you'd better have a sense of humor." He's not alone in his assessment. Robert Half International surveyed vice presidents and human resource directors of 100 large companies. Some 84 percent of those interviewed thought that people with a sense of humor do a better job than people with little or no humor. Employees who could laugh and have fun were most likely to be creative and flexible.

Laughter is a natural tension reducer. Dr. William Fry of Stanford University refers to laughter as "internal jogging." In times of high stress, laughter distracts attention and stimulates the brain to release endorphins, the body's natural morphine-like substance. As laughter subsides, muscles of the body go limp, and the benefits of this relaxation last up to 45 minutes.

Change offers plenty of reasons to be upset, worried, and confused. A manager at a manufacturing plant going through its third restructuring in as many years said to me: "Things are often so emotional around here that I could laugh or I could cry. Crying may be soothing, but laughter is healing."

The playful side of our adult nature has always taken a back seat to the exercise of rational thought. Western society glorifies the philosophy of Descartes: "I think, therefore I am." Am what? Serious, of course. As the English humorist and Member of Parliament Sir A.P. Herbert said ironically, "People must not do things for fun. We are not here for fun. There is no reference to fun in any Act of Parliament." In organizational settings, we are conditioned to suppress our playful minds and to be serious about business. But lately, some leaders are finding tremendous benefit in developing flexible employees through fun and even play.

One of the legendary stories about Sam Walton, founder of Wal-Mart, describes the time he danced the hula on Wall Street. In 1984, Walton made a bet with the CEO of Wal-Mart, David Glass, that the company could not produce more than an 8 percent profit, and that if the company did, Sam would dance the hula. When the company reached the goal, Walton went to New York and found a truckload of authentic hula dancers and a band of ukulele players waiting for him on Wall Street. In addition, Glass had notified the newspapers and television networks, which were there to record the event. Wearing a grass skirt, Hawaiian shirt, and leis over his suit, Sam danced what he described in his autobiography as "a pretty fair hula." Of course, it was hokey, but pictures of the crazy chairman of the board from Arkansas ran in newspapers and on television shows everywhere, and the people at Wal-Mart loved it.

According to the research of W. Jack Duncan, professor and

University Scholar in Management at the Graduate School of Management, University of Alabama, managers who were accepted as friends by employees engaged in the humor network in the same proportion as other members of the team. In other words, when managers initiate jokes and are the target of jokes as much as anyone else, subordinates regard them as colleagues rather than just bosses.

One executive who encourages playfulness in the workplace is Scott McNealy, Sun Microsystem's CEO. The company's infamous April Fool's Day pranks are legend. They began in 1985 when an executive's office was taken apart and reassembled on a float in a nearby fishpond. The prank was widely hailed as a brilliant expression of the company's corporate spirit and it spawned an April Fool's Day tradition at Sun. In 1988 it was the boss's turn. An avid golfer, McNealy arrived at work to find his office transformed into a one-hole, par-four, miniature golf course. Hazards included two sand traps and a bird bath.

University National Bank and Trust (UNB) in Northern California is famous for two things: outstanding customer service and a sense of humor and fun. On the side of the bank building is a cartoon mural of a Martian leaving its spacecraft. Newspaper ads are humorous. Once a year, the CEO offers bags of Walla Walla onions to all customers. At UNB there is no personnel department, yet the bank hires the best talent in the business. Says one happily employed vice president, "The banking business is a small world. We know one another's reputations. And everyone who works here has a list of professional acquaintances who want to join us because we pay well and because it sounds like fun."

It also sounds like fun at Ben and Jerry's, the gourmet ice cream company in Vermont, where Jerry Greenfield (one of the founders) formed a committee that initiated free massages, created an Elvis day, and sponsored a Halloween costume contest. And it certainly was fun for the employees of Convex Computer when Robert Paluck, the CEO, enlivened the annual company picnic by sliding into 72 gallons of iced raspberry Jell-O.

Many organizations consciously make *fun* an integral part of the business. The chairman of AES Corporation, an independent power producer with $500 million in annual sales, actually tracks his employees' job enjoyment. For the past decade, he has surveyed AES employees' fun quotient and itemized the results in the company's annual report. Employees consistently rank their average level of fun at 8 out of a possible 10.

The Body Shop's headquarters, filled with whimsical stuffed sculptures, Seurat prints, and a green pagoda, has been described as looking "a bit like Willy Wonka and the Chocolate Factory." Founder Anita Roddick actively embraces the "playground" image as a means of encouraging employees to lighten up and enjoy their work.

But when it comes to projecting an image of fun verging on lunacy—and making that image pay off—there is no better example than Southwest Airlines. In their book *Nuts! Southwest Airlines' Crazy Recipe for Business and Personal Success,* authors Kevin and Jackie Freiberg offer an example of corporate silliness at its zenith in their account of the 1992 "Malice in Dallas" arm-wrestling tournament between Herb Kelleher, the CEO of Southwest, and Kurt Herwald, the chairman of Stevens Aviation. In the Dallas Sportatorium, before a crowd of employees and the media, Kelleher and Herwald arm-wrestled to decide the user rights to a particular slogan. Rather than engage in a drawn-out, costly legal battle, the executives chose to decide the issue with the best two out of three matches.

The Freibergs set the scene:

> The restless murmur of the crowd, punctuated by the shouts and chants of cheerleaders, crescendoed quickly to hoarse shouts and piercing whistles as, from the darkness at the top of the aisles, the two contenders marched toward the ring. Down one aisle strode Herwald, a burly 37-year-old weight lifter, dressed in slacks and a dark-colored muscle shirt,

wearing a menacing sneer and displaying the tattoo "Born to Raise Capital" on his massive right arm. Down the other, to the hair-raising trumpet blasts of the theme from Rocky, strutted the skinny, white-haired, 61-year-old Kelleher decked out in a white T-shirt, gray sweat pants under shiny red boxing shorts, a sling on his right arm, and a cigarette dangling from his infectious grin, accompanied by a handler wearing a bandolera holding rows of airline-size bottles of Wild Turkey.

Kelleher lost the match, blaming a fractured wrist (injured, he claimed, while saving a little girl from being hit by a bus) combined with a weeklong cold, a stubborn case of athlete's foot, and having accidentally overtrained by walking up a flight of steps. Herwald announced shortly after his victory that he had decided to let Southwest keep using the slogan "Just Plane Smart," and the story became another symbol of the company's zany, irreverent style.

Counterbalance

One definition of the word compensate is "to provide with a counterbalance or neutralizing device." Change-adept individuals compensate for the demands and pressures of business by developing counterbalancing activities in other areas of their lives. They engage in exercise programs and healthful eating habits, they cultivate interests outside of business—sports, hobbies, art, music, etc.—that are personally fulfilling, and they have sources of emotional support. Because employees with counterbalance have a life that includes both work and recreation, they handle stress better and are more effective on the job. Most of all, they have an external source of stability which many refer to as their "anchor" or "rock."

One of the most memorable interviews I conducted on this topic was with the CEO of a cellular telephone company: "I've got one of those 'anchors' in my life. It's my sock drawer." I must have looked startled because he continued quickly. "I mean it," he said. "All hell can be breaking loose at work, but when I come home at night I open my sock drawer to find everything in color-coded, neat little piles. I tell you, it does my heart good."

I've included this story in my speeches for years, and only once has someone taken offense at it. I addressed the national convention of a real estate firm in Florida. A sales manager from California came up to me after the speech and wanted to book a similar program for his division. "I really enjoyed your talk," he said. "But when you speak to my group, please don't make fun of the sock drawer."

I told the sales manager that I would be happy to do as he asked but was curious about the reason for his request. He looked at me sternly. "I don't want you to make fun of it because *it works*. I tell all my salespeople that if they are having a terrible day, where nothing is going right, they might as well go home and straighten out their underwear drawer."

He's right. It doesn't matter if the source of counterbalance sounds silly to others, change-adept people know what works for them.

Leadership Strategy:
Encourage Employees to Work as if Life Mattered

During one of AT&T's many transformations, I interviewed the woman in charge of employee health services to find out what she'd observed about the most resilient people in the organization. I asked her whether she noticed anything that resilient people had in common: Were they employed in a particular geographic region? Had they reached a certain level of the hierarchy? Did they perform similar functions? Were they male or female?

The manager told me that none of those factors made a difference. She said, "People who handle change best in this organization have two things in common: They take good care of themselves and they have outside interests."

As I continued talking with change-adept employees, the same themes kept repeating in my interviews. Those who were most resilient not only had a job—they had a life. Leaders develop change-adept workers when they understand and support the idea of balancing work and life. An executive at Pacific Bell passed on this advice to his staff: "Do not sacrifice your health or your family for any company. Even if the organization treats you extremely well, as it has treated me, it is still not worth trading a life for a career."

Leadership Strategy: Encourage Counterbalance for the Brain

In 1981, Roger Sperry won the Nobel prize for his research with split-brain theory. Sperry studied patients whose corpus callosum (connecting the left and right hemispheres of the brain) had been severed; the results showed that the two sides of the brain perform different functions.

Each hemisphere specializes in distinct types of thinking processes. With 95 percent of all right-handed people, the left side of the brain not only cross-controls the right side of the body but is also responsible for analytical, linear, verbal, and rational thought. When you add columns of numbers, remember names and dates, and set goals and objectives, you are using your left brain. The right-brain hemisphere controls the left side of the body and carries out holistic, imaginative, nonverbal, and artistic functions. When you recall someone's face, become engrossed in a symphony, or daydream, you are engaging in right-brain functions.

A young man once asked management expert Peter Drucker how to become a better manager. "Learn to play the violin,"

Drucker replied. Activities that stimulate the right side of the brain—whether playing a musical instrument, painting pictures, or ballroom dancing—counterbalance an overreliance on left-brain abilities.

Leaders who encourage employees to develop talents that have nothing to do with their jobs find there are unexpected business benefits. The president of CalTex in Kuala Lumpur told me that his company pays for any kind of educational course that employees want to take, the only exceptions being martial arts and cooking classes. He said that the most popular course is singing lessons. This was not totally unexpected because Malaysian employees regularly frequent karaoke bars after work. What he didn't anticipate, however, was the degree to which employees taking singing lessons improved their ability in giving business-related presentations. People conquered stage fright and became comfortable with standing in front of groups. In fact, the only complaint from the president of the company was, "Now they think they can sing!"

Creativity

Buckminster Fuller once said, "Everyone is born a genius. Society de-geniuses them." Change-adept professionals have survived the degeniusing of society to remain curious, creative, and innovative. You can easily spot creative people in organizations. They are the employees who are constantly seeking ways to improve products, services, or themselves. Typically, they questions rules and regulations and contribute ideas beyond the limits of their job descriptions: to other functions, to other departments, and to the organization as a whole. These creative employees solicit diverse opinions that generate new thoughts, and they value any business experience that exposes them to new new knowledge and skills. One project manager summed it up when he said, "If this venture fails, it will still be worth all the time and effort I've put into it for the past 18 months. Just look at everything I've learned!"

Leadership Strategy: Harness the Collective Genius

There was a time when popular opinion held that only a few departments in an organization housed creative people: usually corporate communications, public relations, research and development, and marketing. In the old framework, only top executives were expected to solve problems and develop new concepts. Such a limited view not only placed an enormous burden on the "creative few" to come up with all the answers but also restricted the contributions of workers most knowledgeable about the problem situation. Unleashing the innovative potential in a work force comes only when leadership recognizes the natural creativity that exists within everyone and is willing to remove the tight barriers that restrict the flow of creative ideas.

Creativity is a set of skills that can be developed and applied daily at all levels throughout the organization. A factory peopled by unskilled laborers can benefit from innovative solutions just as much as the most high-powered think tank. For example, a factory employee at Period Furniture, a manufacturing company in Kentucky, devised a solution to problems caused by screws on the plant floor. By installing magnets on the bottoms of all company vehicles, the safety problems and flat tires caused by the dropped screws were eliminated.

Walter Wriston, the former chairman of Citicorp, said, "The person who finds a way to harness the collective genius of the work force is going to blow the competition away." Management today is challenged to take on the role of true leadership and encourage creativity from all employees. As Baldwin's CEO, Karen Hendrix, says, "If I want people to trust me and to be open to my vision, then I must demonstrate that I trust them by being open to their ideas. I have to take a little bit of a leap of faith, myself, and not only entertain ideas from any level of the organization but nurture them with time, resources, and enthusiasm."

Studies show that the biggest stumbling block to employee

creativity at work is the perceived discouragement by management of such activity. If you want to lead an organization to greater heights of creative innovation, make it clear that you want, expect, and value creative input from everybody.

- **Make creativity a part of all job descriptions.** At Mazda in Japan, each employee generates an average of 128.5 suggestions for improvement per year. (Contrast this with the best companies in the United States, whose annual average is 2.3 suggestions per employee.) One of the reasons behind Mazda's prolific idea generation is that workers are told on the very first day of employment that being innovative is part of their job.
- **Gather employee suggestions in "idea campaigns."** The best programs are short term (one or two months), focus on a single issue (improving safety, cutting costs, eliminating paperwork, delighting customers), and are kept lively and fun ("Sacred Cow" hunts to question traditional methods, "Burn the Books" campaign to reduce organizational rules and procedures.)
- **Offer courses in creative problem solving for all employees—not just managers or "creative types."** A study from the State University of New York at Buffalo found that employees who are trained in creative thinking techniques generate twice as many suggestions as untrained employees.
- **Encourage the cross-pollination of ideas.** At 3M, managers regularly organize internal "trade shows" that let different departments share one another's brainstorms and innovations. The result at 3M is a perpetual state of creative competition within the company.
- **Give employees the freedom to be creative.** American Greeting Cards sent a team of its artists to a campsite in the woods—away from the eyes of management—to invent characters that can be used in toys, movies, and comic books. This is a

big change from the days when bosses gave the company artists ideas to work on and the artists were confined to their individual cubicles at corporate headquarters.

• **Reward innovations with private and public recognition.** And if the idea is especially valuable, reward its creator with a cash bonus, royalties, or a percentage of the profits generated by the idea. At ICI Pharmaceuticals Group in Wilmington, Delaware, the Performance Excellence Award is given to employees for any idea that helps the business (saving money, increasing productivity, etc.) or to employees who go "above and beyond" the call of duty. The award winner receives $300. A person can be nominated for this award by anyone: a peer, supervisor, coworker, or department head.

• **Create an environment of trust and information.** Rita Wilson, a senior vice president at Allstate Insurance, spoke with me about the kind of environment needed to encourage creative risk: "We need employees to challenge the status quo, even when that means challenging their assignments. We need them to take responsibility for their jobs and their futures and to contribute creatively to the company's (and their own) success." She added, "We realize that no one can do that unless we create an environment of trust where people feel safe and supported, and unless people also understand the business challenges, goals, and strategies and how their efforts contribute."

Leadership Strategy: Understand the Creative Process

The concept that creativity follows a particular pattern was popularized by Graham Wallace in *The Art of Thought.* In his book, Wallace proposed the following four-step process which should be taught to everyone from whom you expect creative contributions:

1. **Preparation.** In the first part of the creative process, a clear understanding of the situation is established. I refer to this first step as "doing your homework." Creativity does not take the place of logical and strategic thinking—it merely supplements it. Initially, you need to gather all the relevant data, talk to others to broaden your perspective, find out what was tried in the past, and get a sense of the emotions that are embedded in the situation. In a corporate setting, it is also crucial to consider the importance of this challenge in meeting the goals and supporting the values of the organization.

2. **Incubation.** Once the situation is thoroughly defined, the next step is to divert your attention and release the problem from conscious thought. Diverting attention from the problem situation allows the subconscious mind to synthesize and make connections in holistic and intuitive ways that supersede sole reliance on logic.

3. **Illumination.** This is the stage in which you feel a sudden burst of knowledge. The subconscious alerts the conscious through an "ah-ha" experience in which images, thoughts, or understandings break through to awareness.

4. **Verification.** The final step is a "reality check." Is the idea practical, cost-effective, and timely? Can you explain it convincingly? Where can you test it? Can you rally support? What are the most likely objections to be raised by critics? How will you answer the objections?

Leadership Strategy: Look for Multiple Right Answers

As we move into the information age, ideas become the strategic edge for organizations. Innovation and creativity are quickly becoming the keys to corporate productivity and excellence. Never before has it been so crucial for a work force to generate creative ideas.

Linus Pauling, two-time Nobel prize winner, said: "The best way to get good ideas is to begin with lots of ideas." On an airplane trip from San Francisco to Toronto, I sat next to Pauling. I asked him about the greatest obstacle to generating a multitude of ideas, and he replied that it was "any process—educational, scientific, or organizational—that insists on a single right answer." Einstein would have agreed. His thoughts on the subject were captured in one of his famous sayings, "Things should be made as simple as possible, and no simpler."

In today's business world, we are dealing with complex challenges that defy overly simple or one-right-answer solutions. Today there are multiple right answers: A system that works in one department may not be appropriate companywide, successful management approaches in the United States may not work in overseas centers, and leadership skills are most effective when they are situational—adapted to fit different people and circumstances. Continuous improvement is the process by which current right ways constantly transform to become even more effective. As I tell my audiences: "Just remember, there is always more than one right way to deliver pizza, babies, or a joke."

Leaders help employees generate lots of ideas when they ask the following kinds of questions:

- **How would we do it now if we had never done it before?** If we were starting this business from scratch, what are the first things you would do differently? If you could write a new job description, how would you redesign your job? What questions do your kids ask you about work that you can't answer? If you were new to the organization, what questions would you ask?
- **What are a variety of perspectives about this situation?** How does this problem look through the eyes of our customers/suppliers/competitors/the community/people from different departments in the company/people from different

cultures? What are our assumptions about this situation? (Write them down and then write the opposites. Analyze what would happen if the opposite assumptions proved correct.)

- **Which organizational rules are best broken?** Analyze each rule and traditional business practice: What are we doing? Why did we start doing it? Does it still need to be done that way? What would happen if we stopped doing it? What are some better ways of doing it?

- **That's one right answer. What's another?** Help employees move from looking for a single solution to multiple possibilities by embracing the philosophy that there is more than one right way to do business.

Leadership Strategy: Encourage Creative Collaboration

If you and I are in a problem-solving session and we think exactly alike, one of us is redundant. An exercise I use to make this point is a grid of 16 "brainteaser" puzzles. I allow five minutes for people to try to solve the puzzles by themselves, and then I put them into teams to finish the exercise. Before they begin to work together I ask, "What is it that you want from the other team members?" Without fail, the answer comes back: "I want the solutions that I don't already have."

Conformity is the antithesis of creative collaboration. Conformity is what the training film *Brain Power* refers to as "collective ignorance." Creative collaboration, in contrast, is the process of blending diverse opinion, expertise, and perspective into a shared objective. There are many advantages to a diversified employee base, and creative collaboration is high on the list. We need the perspectives, insights, and solutions from people who do not think exactly like we do. We need the answers we don't already have. We need creative collaboration. Leaders build a corporate culture of creative collaboration when they

invite various points of view and utilize the ideas and suggestions of others.

Leadership Strategy: Respect Intuition

When Jonas Salk became a scientist, he pictured himself as a
virus or a cancer cell and tried to sense what it would be like to
be either. I asked Linus Pauling about the value of intuition and
he told me that he once struggled for months with a problem in
chemistry that caught his interest—the reason a certain kind of
anesthesia worked. Seven years later, while walking down the
street thinking of nothing except what a pleasant day it was,
the answer popped into his head fully formed. "Something finally triggered it," he said. "You have to learn to trust your intuition, even if it sometimes takes seven years."

At the New Jersey Institute of Technology, Douglas Dean
studied the relationship between intuition and business success. His findings showed that 80 percent of company executives whose corporate profits more than doubled in the past five
years had above-average precognitive powers. Weston Agor of
the University of Texas in El Paso found that of the 2,000 managers he tested, those at the higher levels consistently scored
higher in intuition.

Andrew Carnegie, John D. Rockefeller, and Conrad Hilton
are historical examples of executives who were known for their
intuitive business decisions. A story about Conrad Hilton high-
lights the value of what was referred to as "Connie's hunches."
There was to be a sealed bid on a New York property. Hilton
evaluated its worth at $159,000 and prepared a bid in that
amount. He slept that night and upon awakening, the figure
$174,000 stood out in his mind. He changed the bid and submit-
ted the higher figure. It won. The next highest bid was $173,000.
Hilton subsequently sold the property for several million dollars.

Traditionally, U.S. employees are schooled to be logical. They are told to rely on numbers and data-collection techniques to solve problems, and so they shy away from intuitive approaches that might be more appropriate. In times of rapid change, analysis is often too slow a tool for decision making. Frequently it is the hunch that defies logic, the "gut feeling" or the flash of insight that turns out to be the best solution.

"Intuition is what you add to the information you collect," said Jan Carlzon of SAS. "If you understand that, you see you can never collect total information. You have to add your feelings and your gut reaction, to make good decisions. In that sense, there is no answer that is right for everybody, just what's right for you. That's using intuition the right way."

A work force that is both highly cognitive and highly intuitive has a distinct advantage in achieving innovative results. Leaders help people in the organization go beyond a purely logical approach to problem solving by acknowledging the validity of emotion, imagination, and intuition.

Leadership Strategy: Entertain Outrageous Ideas

I was hired to facilitate a problem-solving session for a group of 94 male technical workers, none of whom had had previous training in creative thinking. We spent the morning "warming up" with creativity techniques, and in the afternoon the group was divided into teams for brainstorming sessions. By the end of the day, each team was to present its members' ideas to their boss, and he in turn would give authorization and funds to implement the best solutions.

The morning went well when we were all together, but this "creative stuff" was new to everyone, and I was afraid that the isolated teams would revert to the (safer) tried-and-true solutions of the past. To prevent that from happening, I gave a last set of instructions to the group. I reminded them to follow the rules of classical brainstorming:

1. Write all ideas on a large sheet of paper or chalkboard so that everyone can see.

2. Aim initially for quantity, not quality of ideas.

3. "Piggyback" on the ideas of others, adding some new twist to the original suggestion.

4. Hold off judgments and critical evaluation until after all ideas are collected.

Then I added an extra item to the list of instructions. I asked the group to spend the final five minutes thinking of things that would absolutely work but were too expensive, illegal, or in some other way too ridiculous to consider.

When the teams reassembled to present their solutions to the group vice president, each team leader said the same thing: "This started out as our most ridiculous idea, but the more we thought about it, the more it appealed to us. So we found ways to make it our best practical solution."

It is possible to find practical potential in the most outrageous possibilities, but that will never happen in your organization unless leadership is willing to entertain wild ideas in the first place.

Leadership Strategy: Nurture Suggestions and Ideas

An employee at Eli Lilly & Co. suggested a way to recover and reuse the expensive chemical tetrahydrofuran instead of disposing of it as waste, saving the company $708,787 in the recovery program's first year. IBM used an employee suggestion for a tool to mold special computer cable and saved $1.4 million in the first year after inception. A loan manager at Bank of America saved the bank an estimated $363,520 a year just by discovering that there was no need to pay $50 per home loan for property-tax information that could be obtained for free.

What's an idea worth to your organization? Maybe millions? What's the value of harnessing the creative capacity of an entire work force? In a single year at Japan Mazda, 27,000 employees generated 2.7 million suggestions for improvement—an average of 100 ideas from each worker. The company implemented 82 percent of these ideas.

Ideas are elusive and fragile. As a leader who wants to increase the creativity of a work force, the most important question to ask is: How are new ideas treated?

It is easy to discourage creativity by responding to new ideas with such phrases as "We tried it before," "We don't do it that way here," "That's not your job," "We never tried that before, so it's too risky," "Our place is different," or, "It's against company policy." Idea-killing phrases that seek to discourage, diminish, or demean are part of our traditional business culture just as they are part of our upbringing. Consider these reactions to innovative ideas from the past:

- An irate banker once told an inventor to remove "that toy" from his office. That toy was the telephone.
- Harry Warner, president of Warner Brothers, in 1927 commented on the proposal for talking pictures with the remark, "Who the hell wants to hear actors talk!"
- Decca Records pronounced, when it turned down the Beatles in 1962: "Groups with guitars are on their way out."
- The head of MGM studios, Louis B. Mayer, was considering buying the rights to the novel *Gone With the Wind.* His production executive, Irving Thalberg advised, "Forget it Louis, no Civil War picture ever made a nickel."
- Then there was the ultimate discouragement for future innovators, proclaimed in 1899 by Charles Duells of the U.S. Patent Office: "Everything that can be invented has been invented."

If you judge an idea too soon you won't see its full potential. Ideas take time and care to mature. Developing a safe haven for ideas takes a willingness to let ideas emerge freely and to be receptive to them. Nurturing creativity means curbing indifference and harsh criticism so that employees feel free to ask "dumb" questions, challenge rules, and offer novel suggestions.

Leaders who nurture ideas do so by building a relaxed, informal work environment, where rules are deemphasized, employees are encouraged to mix and mingle, and people feel safe in sharing their inspirations with others. Idea promoters respond to new ideas with comments such as the following: "Is this what you meant?" "I appreciate your input." "I don't know if we can do all of it, but I very much like this part of your idea."

Christie Hefner, the CEO of Playboy Enterprises, said:

> Leaders need many of the same things from employees as employees need from leaders: energy and commitment, candor and creativity. But it goes beyond leaders embodying these behaviors to a very basic question: How do you respond when people give you what you ask for? Do you ask people to be honest and then react badly when they tell you the truth? Do you ask for creativity and then punish people when they take reasonable risks? Your responses will determine their behavior.

Some years ago, the world chess champion, Capablanca, played an exhibition match against a New York amateur and lost. Capablanca was renowned for his chessboard strategy—for his ability to plan a dozen or more moves ahead as a game developed—and at the postmatch press conference the amateur was asked how many moves ahead *he* had planned in defeating the master. "Only one," he replied. "The right one."

There, in a nutshell, lies the key to success in a constantly changing world. The amateur chess player wasn't talking about rigidity when he used the word "right." He was talking about flexible, creative reaction, about assessing each position as it developed on the board and then making the move that needed to be made at the moment. He did have an overall game plan, but he didn't frustrate himself trying to anticipate everything Capablanca might do 5 or 20 moves hence. He knew he couldn't outthink the master. So, keeping his basic plan in mind, he tailored his own moves to the immediate possibilities inherent in each position as it arose, and by sticking to that strategy he won a famous victory.

Which is exactly what the most successful corporate leaders do today in response to the constantly shifting and always uncertain facts of life in the modern business world. They work out a general plan for the future, pin it up in the corners of their minds, and then focus on what's happening right now: They assess all the possibilities inherent in each developing situation, decide what needs to be done, and then make the move that will be most advantageous to their company's prosperity and ongoing strength within the parameters of the larger scheme. Sometimes the move is an offensive, attacking one. Sometimes it is a tactical sidestep. Sometimes it is an unexpected counterthrust. But whatever its character and consequence, it is based on the best analysis of immediate circumstances, and it is made in the knowledge that it may well affect the shape of the overall plan to some extent: Every business plan, like every chess game, is fraught with imponderables. Each position has its own unique possibilities and each opponent has his or her own ideas about how to capitalize on them. And remember, in business you aren't just playing against one opponent, you're playing against the whole world. Flexibility, open-mindedness, the capacity to roll with changing circumstances, the ability to absorb and assess new information and to apply it creatively to new situations—those are the strengths of the winning, change-adept company today. As Grandmaster Fred Reinfeld said in *Why You Lose at Chess* (a book every aspiring business leader would do well to study): "You lose because you're stubborn. You have prejudices and preconceived notions, and you refuse to give them up." Unforgivable, Reinfeld concludes, and doubly so in business where there is a good deal more to be lost than just a game.

But in developing your own capacity for flexibility and innovative, change-adept leadership, you have one enormous advantage over the chess player sitting alone at the board. All your chess pieces can think, too. Even the pawns have ideas to contribute. Listen to them. Encourage them. Don't feel threatened or take offense if someone else's ideas prove to be more effective than your own. And don't automatically say "no" if a good ideas falls outside the big plan's borders. In other words, don't think like an old-fashioned boss; think like an enabler. It's the ideas that count, not who came up with them. Find ways to improve your employees' self-confidence and sense of worth. Help them to discover what's positive in challenging situations and how to cope constructively with change. Think about three-dimensional communication, about information that moves simultaneously up, down, and across all layers of your organization with equal facility and openness. Shared knowledge and shared responsibility are what makes businesses work today. Forget about the map on the candy box lid and pass the candy around instead, so that everyone can get a taste of what's there.

CHAPTER 4

Is the Change Finally Over?

Fourth Step: Lead Discontinuous Change

INCREMENTAL VS. DISCONTINUOUS CHANGE

A turnaround is a financial recovery. A transformation is much more. It's all about changing the structure and the approach to business and reeducating our people to feel comfortable outside a command-and-control environment. It involves getting them used to risk taking and innovation. And getting the very best out of our people.

Arthur Martinez, CEO, Sears

Two categories of changes—incremental and discontinuous—are taking place simultaneously in organizations. Incremental change is the process of continuous improvement—what the Japanese refer to as *kaizen*. Author Masaaki Imai calls *kaizen* the single most important concept in Japanese management: "*Kaizen* means ongoing improvement involving everyone—top management, managers, and workers." In Japan, many systems were developed to make management and workers *kaizen*-conscious. According to Imai, one reason why a *kaizen*-driven company is so efficient is that its entire work force is oriented toward spotting new ideas and swiftly and effectively putting them to work.

Incremental change fits the Newtonian framework of linear,

progressive, and predictable change. It uses current practices as a baseline for the systematic improvement of a product, service, or system. There is an unmistakable logic behind incremental change which makes it easy to predict, easy to communicate, and relatively easy for people to adopt. But much of the change our organizations are facing today is not incremental. It is transformative.

Discontinuous change is the kind of large-scale transformation that turns the organization inside out and upside down. If managing incremental change can be compared to encouraging a group of joggers to gradually pick up the pace, then leading discontinuous change is like urging people to leap off a cliff and build their parachutes on the way down. It is no wonder that you can *manage* linear change but you have to *lead* transformation.

Although most leaders are comfortable (and effective) managing incremental change, they are less than effective leading discontinuous organizational transformation. Part of the reason is that discontinuous change—restructuring, reengineering, transformation—challenges our most deeply held beliefs about company well-being. It confronts the entire organization with the possibility that the very roles, actions, and attitudes that were *most* responsible for past success will be insufficient, and perhaps even detrimental, to success in the future. Discontinuous change challenges people at all levels of the organization to take on new roles, new relationships, new values, and radically new approaches to their jobs. But beyond the sheer magnitude of the change itself, and beyond management's often clumsy handling of the "human side" of the process, another overriding reason for the ineffectiveness of large-scale change efforts is that leaders are trying to manage discontinuity with the same linear approach they use with incremental change. And that just doesn't work.

WHY TRANSFORMATION FAILS

I wasn't smart enough about people. I was reflecting my engineering background and was insufficiently appreciative of the human dimension. I've learned that's critical.

Michael Hammer, Author,
Reengineering the Corporation

Only one-third of 1,003 companies that cut employment in the last five years subsequently boosted productivity, according to the American Management Association. Fewer than half boosted profits. And three-fourths of those companies reported declining morale.

In 1993, the Wyatt Company did a study on why corporate restructuring failed. The findings concluded that restructurings failed for one or a combination of the following reasons:

Employee resistance to change	58%
Dysfunctional corporate culture	43%
Inadequate management skills	37%
Lack of line management support	35%
Poor employee communication effort	26%
Lack of senior management visibility	21%
Outside forces intervened (acts of God)	17%
Chose the wrong solution/approach	13%

Only the last item reflects poor strategy and analysis. Restructuring does not usually fail because of poor strategy. The top six reasons are all people issues, and yet most managers still don't understand the human side of the equation. A recent issue of *Fortune* magazine analyzed a nationwide survey on the tactics of reorganization and came to this conclusion: "Most managers don't have as firm a grip on the human aspects of restructuring as they do on finance and technology." A Towers Perrin study on employee attitudes about corporate change produced corroborating results: 68 percent of those queried didn't believe that management was open and honest with them; 58 percent said that communication about change in their organization wasn't given in time; 48 percent said they were not given sufficient information about their company's plans.

It is not that leaders are unaware of the problem. When asked to name the most important skill they need to succeed in the future, leaders almost universally put "managing change" at the top of their lists. It is just that the human aspect—the critical success factor in change management—hasn't been adequately addressed. Consequently, most leaders are still trying to "sell" corporate transformation to employees who are increasingly unwilling to "buy" into it. It is not surprising that so many change efforts are abysmal failures. Under a management that doesn't understand or consider the importance of people's reaction, even naturally change-adept employees will be less eager to embrace transformation.

Organizations don't change. People do—or they don't. Arthur Martinez of Sears has it right when he says, "If you are unable to galvanize people into action, all the thinking, the analysis, the strategic prioritizing doesn't matter at all."

FROM ANSWERS TO QUESTIONS

To repeat: Mobilizing an organization to transform itself to thrive in new business environments cannot be managed with linear strategies. In fact, the best techniques for transformation are not found in *any* formal strategy. Instead, the most effective guidelines to leading discontinuous change *evolve* as leaders reflect on the answers to a series of questions.

Question 1: What Is the Employees' Perspective?

One night at sea, the ship's captain saw what looked like the lights of another ship heading toward him. He had his signalman blink to the other ship: Change your course 10 degrees south. The reply came back: Change *your* course 10 degrees north. The ship's captain answered: I am a captain. Change your course 10 degrees south. To which the reply was: Well, I am a signalman first class. Change your course 10 degrees north. This infuriated the captain, so he signaled back: Dammit, I say change your course south. I'm on a battleship. To which the reply came: And I say change your course north. I'm in a lighthouse!

Like the ship's captain, leaders of discontinuous change can't rely solely on their own points of view. To mobilize a work force for transformation leaders must know what people in the organization are thinking, must encourage them to articulate their points of view and their concerns, and must be ready to respond to them sincerely. The first question that leaders should ask is: "What is the employees' perspective?" And don't rely on secondhand information or make assumptions about what you *think* employees think. *Ask* them—and keep asking them until they tell you:

- What are the complaints you hear most often from customers? (In what ways are we disappointing customers?)
- What are the compliments you hear most often from customers? (In what ways do we please or delight customers?)
- What do you read in the newspapers or hear on the news that concerns you about the future of this company? (Are there rumors/stories about our company or about the industry that worry you?)
- What organizational policies, procedures, or systems get in the way of your doing superior work? (If you could throw out rules that interfere with your performance, what rules would go?)
- What do you like most about working in this organization that you *wouldn't* want to change? (What do you brag about to your friends and family?)
- If we were the competition, how would we outdo ourselves? (What do you personally think about how our products/services compare in value with those of our competitors?)

- What could be done to make your job more exciting? (How would you redesign your job to make it more challenging?

- What trends are going to affect the future of this organization? (What changes have you read about or experienced—in technology, social values, globalization, etc.—that you believe will impact on your job or this organization?)

Everyone in the organization has a special knowledge and sees different needs and opportunities from their particular vantage points. People on the front lines get feedback that comes from working closest to the customer. Technical specialists have early access to technological innovations, and marketers track social and demographic trends. Once you gather the collective insight of the work force and give the entire organization access to it, you may find that the impetus for transformation already exists. And only after you have an understanding of the employees' perspective will you be able to think through this next series of strategic questions:

- In what ways do employees' perceptions already align with yours? (Are their views of customer reactions in line with yours? Do they see the same organizational strengths/weaknesses/challenges that you do? Are they also aware of the trends that you see as the most urgent for the organization? Is there a perception that jobs could be more rewarding with fewer rules—and is that your perspective as well?)

- How can you build on this alignment when leading transformation? (Just as in a negotiation, places of convergent agreement give you a foundation: "We all agree that the customer is disappointed with our speed of delivery." "Most of you think that new technologies are going to allow you to work at least part of the time from your home. I think so too." "Some of you are concerned about the temporary work force we have hired lately. Here are my concerns." Then, whatever you hear from employees, feed back to the entire work force to let every-one know the collective understandings.)

• Where are the gaps between your perception and theirs? (What have employees reported that you haven't considered? Where is your perspective and vision out of alignment with theirs? If, for example, employees say they don't see the threat of international competition—and if this is an area of great importance in your view—you need to know early on that they won't accept competitive pressure as a reason for change unless they are given further evidence.)

Question 2: How Do You Track the Effectiveness of Communication?

As important as it is to find out what employees are thinking before the change, it is just as crucial to have a system for monitoring employees' perceptions throughout the change process. George Bernard Shaw once said that the problem with communication is "the illusion that it has been accomplished." When it comes to communicating change, leadership must be especially careful not to suffer that illusion. *Business Week* made this point in an article about Philips, the Dutch electronics company: "When employees asked at a recent meeting where Philips was headed and why, Timmer (the CEO) was stunned that his troops had failed to comprehend the plan he has tried to hammer home for three years now."

A leader can't afford to wait three years to find that what he or she thought was clearly communicated was, in reality, never understood or believed by the work force. Communication strategies that include a system for employee feedback help organizations track the level of work force comprehension. You will find that the greatest advantages come when organizational feedback is gathered immediately after the delivery of every important message. One of my clients uses this short questionnaire to query her audiences before they leave the meeting room:

- What in your view are the most important points we just covered?
- What didn't you understand?
- With what do you disagree?
- What else do you want to know?

Leaders at Kodak use communication advisory teams (CATs) as both a sounding board for new communications and a feedback system for the effectiveness of current communications. Chosen for their ability to speak up candidly, the members of a CAT represent a vertical slice of the organization. Their primary function is to remark on the quality of communications: What are they hearing? What is their reaction and the reaction of their peers? What questions do they have? Although strictly a management option, another purpose that a CAT can serve is as a preview audience for upcoming corporate presentations and announcements. Leaders can "audition" their speeches: "Here is what I want to talk about. What is your opinion of my style? How is this information going to make people feel?"

A similar communication strategy was developed by consultants at Watson Wyatt. Wyatt discovered that real communication takes place *after* the formal communication—the article in the employee newsletter, the boss's announcement, the video presentation by the CEO—when work group peers seek the reaction of colleagues whose opinions are most influential. Wyatt recommends identifying these peer opinion leaders (POLs) early on and involving them in the design of the communication process for specific issues. The object of this strategy is to immerse these influential peers in the details of the issue so that POLs become a natural "horizontal communication" channel for organizational change.

Question 3: How Do You Get People Ready for the Future?

For a long time we've known that every company goes through a life cycle, from start-up to rapid growth, then into maturity and decline. What's new is that the cycle's time frame, which used to be 10 years or more, is now 2 years or even less. Jack Welch, the CEO of General Electric (GE) says that one of the hardest situations he faces is when an employee asks, "Is the change finally over?" and Welch has to look at the employee and reply, "No. It's only just begun." People need to know why they are being asked to change, and the earlier they have this information, the more time they have to get prepared. They also need to know *why* "change has only just begun." But the most crucial information people must have to prepare for the future is *why the very nature of organizational change has gone from linear steps to discontinuous leaps.* Eastman Kodak CEO George Fisher sees this as his next challenge: "My biggest job over the next two years is not how we develop the market, not even how we gain growth. It is how we get people to start thinking of systemic, rather than incremental change." To prepare people to cope in today's nanosecond world, leaders must adopt a living-systems model that explains discontinuous change as the *natural* process for organizations. Leaders must help the work force look at transformation not as a threat but as exciting, challenging, and desirable.

Question: When will the business stabilize?
Answer: If we're doing it right, it never will.

In most organizations we "Braille the culture," as one professional trends spotter, Faith Popcorn, put it. We run our fingertips along trend bumps as they speed by and try to "read" where we're going. One of the most vital roles of leadership is to anticipate the corporation's future and its place in the global arena and then to formulate strategies for surmounting challenges that have not yet manifested. To proactively respond to these challenges, businesses must continually reinvent themselves. Leaders must encourage employees to constantly question the prevailing business paradigms, and organizations must then act on new opportunities early in the game to maintain a competitive advantage. And when competitors begin to catch up, organizations must be prepared to introduce new products and services that will make their current ones obsolete, even if they are currently successful. To keep in front of the market, organizations must be ready to reinvent themselves every day.

Lewis Platt, the CEO of Hewlett Packard, often states the importance of making your own products obsolete before your rivals do. "We have to be willing to cannibalize what we are doing today in order to ensure our leadership into the future. It's counter to human nature, but you have to kill your business while it is still working."

Effective leaders find ways to anticipate trends and to ride the leading edge of change by dedicating themselves to continual experimentation. But leaders can't be the only proactive members of the organization. They have to alert everyone to changing market realities. When Jack Welch was the head of GE's refrigerator manufacturing division, he put up sheets of paper on the walls of headquarters and kept a highly visible record comparing the production costs and profits of GE with its more successful rival, Westinghouse. After a couple of months, it was clear to all employees that they were facing a situation that would necessitate an organizational change in response. And everyone was ready to undertake it. "The key is to let employees discover the problem," says Jan Carlzon, the former chairman of SAS, "You won't be successful if people aren't carrying the recognition of the problem and the solution within themselves."

More and more leaders are recognizing the need to design and manage a workplace environment that enables people to experience for themselves the need for change. When Susan

Schweizer, manager of a 40-person group that oversees the far-flung telecommunications systems at Digital Equipment Corp., decided that the unit needed to be overhauled, she didn't make any decrees herself. She set up three employee teams to analyze the group's work. After that, she asked the teams to propose how the unit could be better structured to get the work done.

When Rubbermaid held a product fair last year in its head-quarters town, it displayed storage bins, kitchen items, and other plastic housewares, each with a label that detailed what it cost to make and what it sold for. Sounds like a run-of-the-mill corporate event except for two things: The fair was open only to Rubbermaid employees and the products were not Rubbermaid's but its competitors'. Rubbermaid wanted its workers to see for themselves what they were competing against.

The best time to discuss the forces of change is well in advance of the organization's response to them. Leaders develop proactive employees by teaching them to scan the business environment. Everyone in the organization should have a realistic appreciation of the precursors of organizational transformation—the impact of globalization, market fluctuations, technological innovations, societal and demographic changes in the customer base, new offerings by competitors, and new government and regulatory decisions. Employees should also understand how their company, like any living system, thrives on the edge of chaos. Rather than protecting people from outside threats, leaders need to expose workers to the complaints of customers, the new products of international competitors, and the financial reality of costs and profits. Instead of stifling conflicting opinions, leaders must view conflict as the force that drives creativity and learning. To stimulate productive conflict, leaders need to engage the work force in an ongoing dialogue about the most basic business assumptions:

- What business are we in?
- Why are we in business?

- Who are our customers?
- What do our customers want?
- How and where do we best serve our customers?
- Who is our competition?
- How does your current department/job add value to the organization?

In a recent presentation to the Center for the Study of American Business, John Walter, the former president of AT&T, made this observation, "You have to bet on a future that is radically different from the present and the past and drive your own industry, your customers and your marketplace toward entirely new definitions of themselves and their interdependencies." When the rules of competition change, it can happen virtually overnight, and all organizations must stay alert to be able to respond quickly. Federal Express challenged the United States Post Office and changed the "rules" of package delivery, Schwab changed the ways the industry sold stocks and bonds, and Southwest became the most profitable U.S. airline by rewriting the rules about ticket pricing, turnaround time, and what constitutes customer service.

Questions that stimulate strategic speculation include the following:

- What would happen if our current forms of distribution were inaccessible to us?
- What government regulations could "change the rules" of the industry?
- What social trends could cause our customers to stop buying our product or service?
- What kinds of technological innovation would most drastically affect our product or service?
- What changes could the competition (in pricing, services, process, etc.) introduce that would cause us to rethink the way we do business?

- What are the global trends that could most affect our market?
- Under what conditions could this industry become obsolete?

Question 4: How Do You Convince People That Change Is Necessary in Successful Times

There is a story about a frog who was placed in a pot of lukewarm water over a fire which gradually heated the water to boiling. Because the frog failed to notice the point at which the water became hot enough to kill it, it stayed in the pot and was cooked. The danger of organizational success is that, like the warm water, it can lull us into a comfortable complacency that dismisses the signals of threat.

Traditionally, organizations in North America changed in response to crisis. When Ford Motor Company restructured in the 1980s, it was in response to a record financial loss, $3.3 billion from 1980–1983. Although it was a devastating event, this crisis served as a self-evident rationale for change. The corporation's old strengths—a rigid hierarchy and specialization of labor at all levels—became a weakness. A way of doing business that served Ford well for decades no longer applied; Ford had to change to survive. And the company learned from that experience. One of the things it learned was to change *before* it was forced to. Ford's 1995 global restructuring, "Ford 2000," was developed when the company was in good financial health, with 1994 pretax profits of $5.3 billion. This time the change was not made in response to crisis but from a position of strength and on the basis of considered judgments about future needs and aims.

Today our organizations are dealing with forces that are so dynamic and fast moving that to wait until there is proof of crisis is to respond far too late. The way that the accelerated pace of change drastically shortens response time was once explained to me in the following manner: If I was walking down the middle of a residential street and I saw a car coming at me from a couple blocks away, there would be plenty of time to get to the sidewalk, but if I were in a jet plane heading for another jet plane traveling at the speed of sound, even two miles wouldn't be far enough away to react in time to avert a collision.

Success brings another, and even more insidious danger to our organizations—the belief that we have now found the right way to do things. And when people strongly believe they are *doing it right,* it's almost impossible to make them consider alternative possibilities.

For centuries, people believed that Aristotle was right when he said that the heavier an object, the faster it would fall to earth. All it would have taken to disprove Aristotle was for one brave person to take two objects of different weights and drop them from a great height to see whether or not the heavier object landed first. But no one stepped forward until nearly 2,000 years after Aristotle's death. In 1589, Galileo summoned a group of learned professors to the base of the Tower of Pisa. Then he went to the top and pushed off a 10-pound and a 1-pound weight. Both landed at the same time. But the power of belief was so strong that the professors denied what they saw and continued to insist that Aristotle was right!

All this points to the difficulties leaders face when, at the height of the organization's success, they still ask their work force to examine every basic assumption and business practice and to prepare to abandon much of what made them successful in the past. This difficult and delicate leadership task often leaves workers disgruntled ("What *more* do they want from us?") and leaders frustrated by the lack of employee enthusiasm.

To transform a successful organization, a leader must provide direction and the rationale for change by identifying future challenges and clarifying business realities. Leaders of enterprises must be able to view business patterns as if they were looking down from a rooftop. Leaders should give employees a strong sense of the history of the enterprise and what was especially good about its past, as well as a clear idea of the market forces at work today and the responsibility people must take in shaping the future of the enterprise. And, once again, the leader's role in this process must shift from supplying slick solutions to framing key questions and bringing critical issues into corporate awareness.

One of the most effective strategies to convince employees to change when times are good utilizes proactive problem solving ("What are the future challenges that we need to begin preparing for today?") coupled with status quo risk analysis ("What is the risk of trying to stay competitive in this dynamic business environment with the organizational status quo?"). When management and employees honestly address these issues, people in the organization can understand a basic reality: Regardless of your current level of success, in volatile times the greatest risk of all is not to change.

Question 5: Do You Give Honest Answers to Tough Questions?

In a study of hundreds of workers, Jim Kouzes, a management professor, asked: "What trait do you look for in a supervisor?" With incredible consistency, respondents gave first preference to honesty. It is no coincidence that I also found openness and honesty reiterated as essential ingredients for communicating change. In the light of economic realities that offer little in the way of job security, employees must be able to rely on their employer to give them honest information that will allow them to make informed choices about their own jobs, careers, and futures.

The need for candor starts even before a person is hired. A study of corporate recruitment practices by M.E. Scott, a recruitment consulting firm, found that the most effective practices are those that offer job seekers candid, detailed, job-specific information. More than elaborate promises, applicants mainly want to know what it will be like to work at a company. It is important to accurately portray job requirements—both the positive and the negative aspects—to the candidate. An equally candid description of the organization's culture will help a prospective employee form realistic expectations and will increase the likelihood that the person will feel satisfied once on the job. When employers share strategic objectives, even new recruits are able to develop a sense of purpose as they begin to understand the business issues and what the company is trying to achieve.

Not only can employees tolerate large amounts of candor, they are increasingly demanding it. At a recent speaking engagement for a national bank, I asked the program coordinator what issues she wanted me to address. "Just give us the facts," she said. "We want to hear the unadulterated truth, as you see it." I've come to believe that this is also what employees most want from their leaders. Certainly at the beginning of any large-scale transition, employees want straight answers to these tough questions:

- Will I keep my job?
- How will pay and benefits be affected?
- How will this affect my opportunities for advancement?
- Will I have a new boss?
- What new skills will I need?
- What will be expected of me?

Until these personal issues are resolved, employees are too preoccupied with their own situation to pay much attention to meeting the needs of the organization. It is advisable to meet these sensitive issues head on and volunteer to let people know where they stand. If leadership does not address these workplace concerns, the company rumor mill will speculate, gossip, embellish, trade half-truths, and generally elevate the work force's anxiety level.

When you can't answer every question, it is best to tell people that you understand their concern but don't know the answer. Or, that you don't have the information yet but will get back to them as soon as decisions are made. It is even better to tell people that you have the information but can't release it than to withhold or twist the truth. Not everyone will appreciate candid communication, but few will tolerate anything less.

During a major organizational restructuring, West Texas Utilities (WTU) published the minutes of every meeting of the change-management task force and let all employees see how decisions were being evaluated and made. At first, the leadership at WTU thought so much candor might increase work force resistance, but it soon became apparent that the more employees knew about the inner workings of the task force, the more readily they accepted the change proposed.

Question 6: What's in It for Them?

I was in Sweden working with a county government agency that was completely revamping its health care system. The leader of this enormous change was proud of the way he had communicated to the county's residents. They had been given a thorough briefing: the reasons behind the change, the timing of the change, and exactly how it was to be carried out. Then he turned to me with a frown, "But you know, there is still one question that I get asked all the time." I interrupted. "Let me guess," I said. "People want to know if the wait for a doctor's appointment will be any shorter than it currently is. Am I right?" The man looked startled. "How did you know that?" he asked. I told him that I knew to expect that question because it is the one I hear most often about change: What's in it for me?

When it comes to discontinuous change, this is not always an easy question to answer, but it is much easier to approach if the work force is prepared to expect constant transformation as the natural process of growth. If that groundwork was laid well in advance, you can talk openly about the personal benefits of becoming proactively involved in the change process. Here's how I dealt with this question in a speech I gave to a management group in Canada:

> While doing background research for this program, I came across a newspaper item from 40 years ago. It seems that until the mid-1950s, Canadians had never held an Easter parade, so the city fathers announced that at 10 A.M. on Easter Sunday the first event of this kind would take place. The citizens of Toronto arrived promptly at 10 o'clock, lined the sidewalks of the main street, and waited for the parade to begin. They waited all morning, and no parade was ever spotted. Disappointed and angry at what they assumed was some sort of municipal hoax, the people went home. What the people of Toronto failed to realize is that an Easter parade wasn't something you watched—it was something you *did.* Everyone, dressed in their finest clothes, took the arm of others similarly attired and "paraded" down the center of the street.

The reason I tell this story to employees is to get them to think about their future in the changing organization as an Easter parade. It's futile to wait on the sidelines. They've got to jump in—to take an active role in the change process—and create a future they deserve.

David Kearns, the former CEO of Xerox Corporation, says that the single most important thing an organization can do to ensure its success in the future is to find ways to make change a motivator rather than a demotivator. Leadership strategies that help motivate employees to change include the following:

• **Creating a positive vision of the organization's future.** Walter Blankley, the CEO of AMETEK, puts it succinctly: "Leaders motivate others to see the advantages in change by providing a vision and a mission that everybody understands, relates to, and is connected to."

• **Using real life examples of others who have benefited during a similar change.** When planning an organizationwide change, begin it in one department or division so that you can use the success stories of people who found personal advantages—learning and growth opportunities, increase in self-confidence, more job satisfaction—in the process.

• **Helping people discover personal advantages.** There are personal advantages to be found in almost every change, but sometimes people need help discovering what the advantages are. Sometimes employees just need someone to guide them through a few questions: What are your career goals? What are the skills you would like to learn? What job-related experiences you would like have? In what ways might this change help you to fulfill some of your personal objectives? (It might be the chance to learn how to use new technology, the experience of serving on a change task force, an opportunity to make suggestions for improvements outside your usual work area, a chance to be cross-trained in other, needed skills, etc.).

• **Linking employees' participation and contribution to the rewards of success.** The leaders at Honeywell have some pretty aggressive goals for the year 2000: to become a $10 billion company, to be on *Fortune* magazine's list of most-admired companies, and to increase employee stock ownership to 15 percent. To achieve these goals, Honeywell is engaging its work force in a "value creation cycle" in which employees create value in the company and share in success they've created. And here is where Honeywell's concept of linkage comes in: Gone are the days when executives took sole responsibility for Honeywell's financial performance. Today, employees' knowledge of how the business works and how their activities affect the company's success is seen as crucial to achieving goals. Employees are informed about Honeywell's objectives and priorities, asked to see themselves (and each other) as equal partners with customers and shareholders, and educated to understand the financial side of the business. And as the company grows, employees share in the success through variable pay (a portion of their pay that varies with the company's performance) and higher stock value.

Question 7: Is Your Communication "Behavior Based"?

In San Francisco, on the corner of Powell and Market, street performers entertain tourists as they wait for the cable car to arrive. My favorite "act" is two fully dressed men who spray-painted themselves gold and silver. Posing like statues, they kneel on the sidewalk facing each other with their elbows resting on a low platform and hands clasped in a traditional arm-wrestling position. In front of the man painted gold, there is a gold hat. In front of the silver man is a silver box. They stay absolutely motionless, until someone in the crowd puts a coin or a bill in one of the receptacles. If the money goes into the gold hat, the gilded man inches his arm forward gaining a slight advantage in the "wrestling match." They hold the new position and wait. If money goes into the silver box, then the silver man makes a move. All this is done in total silence. Neither man looks at or speaks to the audience. They don't ask for money, and there is no sign instructing people about the procedure for or the result of making a contribution, yet the audience understands almost immediately what they are supposed to do. This is the essence of behavior-based communication.

Corporate leaders are beginning to learn the importance of behavior-based communication as a requirement for leading discontinuous change. Organizations send two concurrent sets of messages about change. One set of messages goes through formal channels of communications—speeches, newsletters, corporate videos, values statements, and so forth. The other set of messages is "delivered" informally through a combination of "off-the-record" remarks and daily activities. For today's skeptical employee audience, rhetoric without action quickly disintegrates into empty slogans and company propaganda. In the words of Sue Swenson, the CEO of Cellular One, "What you do in the hallway is more powerful than anything you say in the meeting room."

Basically, behavior-based communications is a five-step process:

Step 1. Determine your current "values alignment." Create a "say/do" survey to find the gaps between what employees hear the organization say and what they see the organization do: Here is what our values state . . . What actions do you see us taking that are in alignment with our values? What behaviors are not in alignment?

Step 2. Communicate company actions *to tell a common story to your stakeholders.* Focus on business processes and practices that collectively define the corporation to employees, customers, shareholders, and communities. Few companies are better at this than Nordstrom, which uses the *same stories* of employee dedication to customer service to communicate their values inside and outside the company.

Stee 3. Link action examples to all key messages you communicate formally. (The crucial questions to ask as you plan the communication process are: What does this mean in a behavioral context? What do we need to do to demonstrate this?) I advise leaders to go even further and ask: What actions can we take *first* to be used as examples in the formal communication? (This is what I refer to as the "talk your walk" approach.) If a company wanted to communicate its commitment to team building, I'd recommend holding off any corporate announcement until leadership fully understood how their behavior had to change to be perceived as supportive of the team concept, until there was a system developed for teaching team-building skills to employees and a process for educating managers as team coaches, and until there was an appropriate shift from individual to team accomplishments in rewards and recognition programs.

Step 4. Create the corporate mechanisms that bring values into action. 3M allows scientists to spend 15 percent of their time working on whatever interests them, requires divisions to generate 30 percent of their revenues from new products introduced within the past four years, has an active internal venture capital fund, and grants prestigious awards for innovations. I don't know if 3M has a formal "values statement," but I know what they value.

Step 5. Track your progress. Alexian Brothers Hospitals have an executive with the title Vice President of Mission Effectiveness, whose job is to make sure that the alignment between organizational values and actions remains intact.

Question 8: Do You Harness the Power of Symbols?

Stanley Gault of Goodyear Tire and Rubber Co. made a lot of changes since becoming CEO in 1991. One of his top priorities was to reduce costs. Many of the actions he took started with him—like selling off the company's limousine fleet and five corporate jets. The example that people like best, however, involves light bulbs. As a symbolic gesture, Gault went around his office suite and removed 25 light bulbs from wall sconces, lamps, and chandeliers. He calculated that reducing the number of light bulbs in his office saved the company $230 a year. After he got rid of his own light bulbs, lights were turned out in halls and offices all over the company.

Other business leaders used symbols and symbolic gestures with equal success:

- At SAS, Jan Carlzon publicly burned thousands of pages of manuals and handbooks to demonstrate the extent to which rules and procedures had become overdominant in communicating company goals and policy.
- When Fred Gibbons, CEO at Software Publishing, wanted to create a more egalitarian workplace environment, he removed the door to his office, eliminated special parking privileges, and saw to it that all company desks were the same size.
- In Europe, the style of company car an executive drives is

a symbol of rank and privilege. During a restructuring that included employee cutbacks, the executives of a large manufacturing company in England exchanged their fleet of Mercedes for Volvos. (On the day of delivery, the cars were prominently displayed in the front row of the company parking lot.) The signal to employees was that everyone was affected in some way by the negative impact of cost cutting.

Symbols can be potent agents for change, but symbols can also work against you. In early 1991, during a contract dispute with pilots, CEO Robert Crandall took out full-page ads in national newspapers titled "AApology," asking passengers to have patience with the carrier while pilots were conducting an illegal sickout to force flight cancellations. Infuriated pilots, who dispute that a sickout ever took place, still carry key chains with the text of the ad laminated underneath. That's a powerful symbol of a six-year grudge that even today affects management–labor relations at American.

Question 9: What's the Little Picture?

A few years ago I was invited to speak at a function where top management was introducing a new corporate vision to initiate an organizational restructuring. It was quite an event. The goals of the organization were written out in calligraphy on parchment paper and distributed to the 1,200 middle managers in the audience. The stage was decorated with an artistic backdrop—a shield with all the important corporate values symbolically displayed. I was the opening speaker. The CEO followed me. Several other senior executives spoke, and then we all sat back and congratulated each other on a job well done.

At the luncheon that followed, a friend of mine from the audience came up to me. "What did you think of the new corporate goals?" she asked. "Right on target," I responded enthusiastically. "And what about our values?" she continued.

"Inspiring," I assured her. "I thought so too," she said. "Only one thing, though. We've been sitting in the audience all morning waiting for one of you to explain how we can possibly *do* all that."

We hadn't inspired that audience with the big picture—we'd overwhelmed them. It was a lesson I've never forgotten.

Vision is the big picture, and it is crucial to the success of the enterprise, but along with the big picture, people also need the little picture:

Big picture: Presenting the concept of transformation
Little picture: How are we going to do that?
Big picture: Setting long-term corporate goals
Little picture: Where do we begin?
Big picture: Developing the overall objectives of the transformation
Little picture: What are the priorities?
Big picture: Creating the mission of the organization
Little picture: Where does my contribution fit in?
Big picture: Communicating organizational values
Little picture: What does this mean in my daily life?

The shift from an internal focus to a customer focus at British Airways took place over four to five years, and its leadership prioritized and sequenced the rate of change. The most important issues were dealt with in succession: building a credible executive team, communicating with a highly fragmented organization, defining new measurements of performance and compensation, and developing sophisticated information systems. During each step, employees at all levels were helped to identify what and how they themselves needed to change to make the transition work for everyone.

Question: How do you eat an elephant?
Answer: One bite at a time.

Question 10: Whose Vision Is It?

Leaders understand the power of vision to imbue people with a sense of purpose, direction, and energy. A compelling vision of the future pulls people out from the seductive hold of the past and inspires employees to set and reach ambitious corporate goals. Of even greater importance is the sense of meaning that people derive from their jobs when they can tie their contributions to the fulfillment of a clear, compelling vision. Therefore, leaders must be able to paint the big picture. But if the vision belongs only to top management, it will never be an effective force for transformation. The power of a vision truly comes into play only when the employees themselves have had some part in its creation. So the crucial question becomes, "Whose vision is it?"

When the 20 top executives go on a retreat to discuss the meaning of work and the future of the organization, they may return with a meaningful, well-crafted vision statement. But when they present this vision to their company, employees seldom find anything to connect with personally because they were never part of the discussion. If you want employees to feel the same kind of connection to their work that the executives felt at the retreat, you have to get employees involved too. And when you involve people in creating a vision of the organization, their statements reflect a deeper meaning than any leader would dare conceive: Chemical workers at DuPont in West Virginia created a statement that began: "We will make West Virginia, the United States, and the world a safer place."

So go off on a retreat to find your vision for the organization and the meaning in your work. Then talk about what you did and how you did it and invite everyone to make the vision come alive for them by discussing, aligning with, and owning it. This can be accomplished in three simple steps:

1. Each department reviews the corporate vision as it was conceived by top leadership. (For example, a hospital's

executives create a vision of "providing the best health care in the industry at the lowest cost." The executives communicate the vision throughout the hospital.)

2. Departments discuss how their specific functions support the overall vision and objectives. (The head of the hospital meets with the maintenance department to talk about the importance of cleanliness in reducing chances of infection and aiding patient recovery. The department discusses the specific ways in which what they do affects the hospital's goals of patient care and cost containment.)

3. Departments create their own vision, which aligns with corporate vision. (The maintenance department creates its personal vision of "providing the best professional cleaning service in the most efficient manner.")

The Ritz-Carlton's president, Horst Schulze, says it's not enough for employees to simply perform their functions. "For new staff, the idea is first to let them know what we are all about and where we are heading. Then each person discusses what he wants to do and we help him set up his personal goal and to develop a vision for himself."

Question 11: Are You Emotionally Literate?

To be a consummate communicator of change it is not enough to engage people's logic, you also have to employ the power of emotion. When Lou Gerstner first joined IBM as CEO, he was asked why he spent so much time traveling to make personal appearances at numerous IBM facilities. He answered: "You've got to appeal to people's emotions. They've got to buy in with their hearts and bellies, not just their minds."

As companies arrive at the insight that people skills—almost universally called the "soft stuff" of business—hold the key to organizational change, human emotions take on new significance. Increasingly I am asked to consult with senior management to help them address the emotional turmoil that the work force experiences around change. And it takes just a quick look at the recent past of corporate America to see how the work force has been conditioned to respond so negatively. Look at it from the employees' point of view: The company is restructured, maybe merged with or taken over by another firm. All top management is replaced. There are massive layoffs, followed by rumors of more personnel cuts to come. No one knows the direction of the new organization or whom to turn to for guidance. Employees suffer "survivor guilt" and struggle under added workloads. People see dedicated coworkers being fired while on vacation, through messages left on answering machines, even in front of their children on "bring your daughter to work" day. And from this emotionally damaged body, the work is still expected to flow as if nothing happened and employees are expected to eagerly embrace the next announced change.

Negative emotional reactions spring from outrage and fear:

> "First of all, you see the wrong people getting cut. You know some of these people; they worked hard and did a good job for the company."
> "They never even warned us. I had to read about the layoffs in the paper."
> "The way they treated people was awful—with no concern for their feelings. At first I was relieved to be keeping my job, but then I started thinking that it could just as well have been me."
> "I really felt sorry for my friends who were fired, but now I think they may have been the lucky ones."

Leaders who continue to think of change as a purely logical event will never understand the psychological pain that it generates in the work force. I remember one research project I conducted for a regional president who had recently taken on his new position. "I am replacing a man who was with the company for 20 years." he said. "I'm new to the organization and I'd like you to find out what employees need from me as their leader."

A week later I gave him my report. "I think you're going to like what I found," I began, "because what employees need most won't cost you anything. People aren't asking for additional pay or more support. What they are waiting for—and what they want from you more than anything else—is an acknowledgment of their distress." The employees in his division were waiting for someone to say to them: "My God, you've lost a leader who was your friend, mentor, and model. What a difficult time you must be having!"

Large-scale organizational change almost invariably triggers the same sequence of emotional reactions—denial, negativity, transition, tentative acceptance, commitment. Leadership can either facilitate this emotional process or ignore it—at the peril of the transformation effort.

Denial

If the organization is *insufficiently prepared* for the reality of discontinuous change, people's initial reaction is usually shock and denial. People in shock are emotionally numb and refuse to believe the change will take place. Informal conversations around the company begin with remarks such as the following: "It will all blow over, it's just a matter of time," or, "They'd never do that to us." At IBM, denial manifested in a "mainframe mindset"—the blind insistence that in spite of the emergence of personal computers, big computers would reassert their market dominance. This reaction is not only to be anticipated in business enterprises but can also occur in other populations. In one of my seminars for Chamber of Commerce executives, a participant reported that, in his city, people still spoke about the mining industry making a comeback. The mines had been closed for 20 years.

Because employees in denial refuse to believe the change will occur, there is little observable difference in their behaviors and attitudes, so it is easy for management to get the mistaken impression that people are having no difficulties handling the new situation. This is an inaccurate impression, of course— what appears to be acceptance of change is actually emotional numbness accompanying the shock of disbelief. If employee reaction to the announcement of a major change seems surprisingly passive, start asking questions!

In dealing with denial, leaders are faced with the challenge of making sure that all employees understand that the change is important, real, and imminent. If the key to the success of a real estate venture is "location, location, location," the key to dealing with denial is communication, communication, communication. Leaders need to stay visible and approachable while getting their message out in every medium at their disposal. Some employees are visual and don't believe it until they see it in print or on their computer screens. Some are auditory and want to hear about change from top executives and again from their direct supervisors, and still others won't believe it until they see it in action. So, speech material, articles in in-house publications, stories in the press, videotapes, electronic mail, satellite conferences, and, most especially, organizational behaviors should all be part of a unified communication campaign that reinforces the need for transformation and offers a vision of the organization's future. And remember, it is most important to address the most basic questions: Why are we changing? When are we changing? How are we changing? What are we changing? What *isn't* changing? How does this change fit into the overall vision? How does it affect *my* life?

Negativity

When people move through the numbness of denial, they usually begin to have negative feelings—self-doubt, fear, sadness, self-pity, depression, frustration, anger, grief, and even hostility. At this point things seem to get worse. Typical responses include the following:

"I'm not going to put up with this without a fight,"
"How could they do this to me after all I've done for them?"
"What will I do if I get laid off?"
"I'm powerless, so I might as well give up."

Whether combative or outwardly compliant, employees worrying about the personal impact of change or made resentful by the layoff of colleagues have a hard time focusing on their jobs. During this phase of intense emotional reaction, managers can expect absenteeism and mistakes to rise as productivity and morale decline.

Negativity is the most difficult emotional component for managers to deal with, but it's a natural part of the transformation process and must be faced. Leaders will find that it is counterproductive to ignore negative feelings, to punish employees for their "disloyal" attitude, or to attempt to "cheer up" people who are in obvious distress. What works best is to allow sufficient time for the reality of the proposed transformation to sink in and then to schedule planning sessions to openly discuss employee concerns and feelings. Although you may not have a degree in psychology, don't be surprised if you feel that some of your meetings have turned into therapy sessions with *you* as the therapist. By creating a safe place for people to express concern and criticism without judgment or fear of the consequences, you are helping them break through the negativity. By asking for, listening to, and addressing differing perspectives, leaders show that they are connected to the real world of the employee and that their own decisions are based on an understanding and evaluation of all sides of a situation.

Resistance to change should be anticipated and encouraged. Unexpressed negativity does not disappear, it goes underground to resurface later, often sabotaging an operation after the organization has made substantial investments in time, money, and manpower. If management encourages a frank dialogue about fears and reservations early on, there is time to revamp systems to better support the change, intensify communication efforts, generate more employee involvement, develop strategic alternatives, or (occasionally) even to jettison an unpopular plan. A forthright discussion also affords employees the opportunity to distinguish between those aspects of the change that might be able to be altered and those that are seen as central to the goals of the organization. If nothing else, encouraging people to express dissatisfaction lets them know that it is safe to disagree with management, that their concerns are being heard, and that their ideas and feelings are important. And, by the way, if you can't facilitate this sort of process well yourself, it's a good idea to bring in someone who can.

The beginning of anything new always means the death of the old. Changing the way work gets done means employees have to give up the competence and confidence they gained under the old system. Employees under new leadership must relinquish the relationships they created with their previous boss. A work force relocating to new facilities has to leave behind the old building. With every "death" comes a period of mourning when people grieve for what they are being asked to leave behind. This is why you can expect that employees in the midst of a cultural transformation are almost certain to take a nostalgic look back at "the good old days" and to mourn the passing of that familiar culture.

Leaders of discontinuous change must focus on the future without describing the past as wrong. It is unproductive to tell people that they must change to "correct" their past performance. It is also unrealistic to speak of "correcting" when the past was highly successful. But, in any case, it is wise to assume that workers did their best in the past. Telling them it was not good enough—that, in effect, *they* were not good enough—is demoralizing, demotivating, and guaranteed to build resentment.

Instead of blaming the old ways, leaders can help employees detach from the past by allowing them to mourn it. To facilitate people through the mourning period, the past must be honored in an almost ritualistic sense. From pictorial displays on company walls to parties celebrating the history of the organization, rituals help people say good-bye and move on.

Even employees going through an emotionally devastating situation, such as the closing of a plant, want to have the past honored. After more than a century of operation in the Lehigh Valley of Pennsylvania, Bethlehem Steel Corporation stopped making steel in its home city on November 18, 1995. The plant management team commissioned a video to commemorate the facility and pay tribute to the people who had worked there—in many cases three and four generations of one family. The video was mailed to 2,900 active employees during the week the operations were closing. In a hostile labor–management environment, where 1,800 jobs were lost, only three people either refused to accept the video or returned it to management.

I don't mean to suggest that a commemorative video is the cure-all for employees' distress over losing jobs and closing facilities. But if those events are facts over which plant management has no control, the question becomes how to deal with human beings facing the consequences of those facts. Management can either ignore people's suffering (the easier, less risky, management choice) or confront it by paying tribute to the past. And, in fact, in the case of Bethlehem Steel, almost all employees were uniform in their praise for the video as a lasting memento and for its sensitivity to the subject and the people.

When Federal Express acquired Flying Tigers Airline,

FedEx added a wing to its corporate museum to show the history of Flying Tigers. Then Fred Smith, the CEO, flew the pilots of the acquired company to Memphis where they visited the museum and viewed the exhibit. Smith knew that the pilots were mourning the loss of their company, and he wanted to acknowledge their grief and honor their past success.

Another famous acquisition (Western Airlines by Delta Airlines) is described by Rosabeth Moss Kanter in her book, *When Giants Learn to Dance.* A period of mourning was encouraged to help people bury the past. This process included testimonials that were written by longtime Western employees and distributed to all employees. Delta even held a kind of wake at which each of the Western people attending were asked to write down the three worst things that could happen to them as a result of the merger. Also, Western managers were each given several pieces of their former letterhead and business cards and were led outside and assembled around a wooden casket. As a band played the funeral march, one by one each person was asked to crumple up their statements, cards, and letterhead and toss them into the coffin. When they were finished, a 100-ton paver came rolling around the corner. As it approached the coffin, the band burst into the spirited tune "On Wisconsin," and the group cheered as the paver rolled over the coffin, flattening its contents. As soon as this ceremony was over, the group was taken back inside, given caps and gowns to wear, and assembled in the meeting room. Each manager was then called forward and awarded a "Doctorate in Merger Management" certificate and a share of Delta stock. Only then did the president of the company make his "Welcome to Delta" speech.

Hokey? Sure. But we're all a little hokey when it comes to what touches us emotionally.

Transition

The transition point is a period of vacillating emotions as people in the work force choose whether or not to support the transformation. There is a tremendous cleavage in organizations going through transition, as the more change-adept employees move into new roles and relationships while others stand firm in their opposition—which leaves the undecided majority feeling much like the taffy in a taffy pull. The schizophrenia of going through a transition is expressed by people's comments:

> "Maybe this will be for the best, but on the other hand . . ."
> "I'm not sure that I can meet the new challenges, but
>   perhaps . . ."

Leaders help employees through transition by giving them honest information about requirement for future success within the organization. It is important to discover and tell the stories of company "heroes"—those workers whose behaviors exemplify success under the new model. (If you are transforming the organization to be more customer-responsive, have customers rate your service on a scale of 1 to 10, and make an example of the first team of employees who receive a score of 8 or higher.) The benefits of communicating employee success stories are twofold: First, it is an opportunity to recognize and reward the change adept, who have already embraced transformation. Second, it provides all employees with real-life examples of theory moving into practice by showing what it takes to be successful.

It is also important for each individual to assess his or her skills in light of the current job market. Those who have been with the company for a long time are probably unaware of what is available to them in the wider employment world. A thorough assessment of their skills and aptitudes can prepare employees for making good choices within the new structure.

As people consider letting go of the past, they will be looking for something to replace their losses. The leader's role is to create *linkage* between the transformed corporation and its employees. The concept of linkage goes beyond making sure that everyone knows where the company is headed, what's expected of them, and how their contributions fit into the overall strategy—although all those concepts are vitally important. True linkage—the kind that bonds committed employees to the success of the organization—comes when there is alignment between the values of the company and those of the work force. As a leader, the most effective way of developing this powerful linkage is to encourage employees to clarify their own personal goals and values and to see how they fit within the vision of the transformed organization.

Linkage Exercise

Step 1: Define your personal values.
   How do you define success in life?
   How do you want to be remembered?
Step 2: Decide what your professional "purpose" is.
   What do you want to accomplish in your career?
      Why?
   What are you passionate about achieving?
Step 3: Write out your goals.
   What are your professional goals for this year?
   What are your professional goals for the next five
      years?
Step 4: Describe your ideal working environment.
   Under what working conditions are you the happiest
      and most productive?
**Step 5: Write out the values and principles of the
   organization.**
   What attitudes and behaviors does the company
      value?
   What organizational principles would you be fired for
      violating?

Step 6: Link your goals and values to the organization.
How do the values of the organization reflect your
own values?
How do the changes going on within the company
afford you new opportunities to reach your goals?

There is no single organizational culture and no universal
set of corporate values that is right for every worker. I've interviewed employees in paternalistic companies who were uncom-
fortable with paternalism: "I wish they'd stop calling this a
family. It isn't. It's a business. But that doesn't mean we still
can't treat each other with caring and respect." I've talked with
highly paid workers in Fortune 500 organizations who felt lost
in an anonymous sea of faces: "I'd love to work for a small company where I knew my contribution really mattered." And I've
heard the opposite lament from employees working in home of-
fices for entrepreneurial start-ups: "I really miss the interaction
of meeting face-to-face with members of a team. I wish I were
with a big, bustling enterprise." The idea is not to try to become
all things for all employees but, rather, to have your culture so
well defined and promoted that employees looking for a values
match know exactly what they are getting.

One of the most emotionally distressing situations is created
when people try to thrive in a business environment that
doesn't support their principles or goals. And if that alignment
is seriously askew, the best thing for both the organization and
the employee would be to help the worker find a new job in a
different organization. But the need to sever the current business relationship is less frequent than you might expect. The
purpose of a linkage exercise is to help employees make connections between their goals and beliefs and the opportunities
the organization offers. An unexpected research result of using
this exercise in hundreds of companies was finding that regardless of the outcome, the very process of clarifying personal values and goals caused employees to be more supportive of their
organization.

Acceptance

Once people agree to support the change, they are ready for action. Organizations in the early stages of the acceptance phase are characterized by abrupt increases of energy and enthusiasm. Informal conversations will begin with: "I've got another idea," "Where do you suppose this might fit in?" "How do we get started?" The management challenge at this point is to focus and channel this energy by restating the overall vision and giving employees access to all information needed to understand the dynamics of the transformation and to emphasize the need to collaborate with others and to experiment with various solutions. It may feel as though you are starting over from the beginning—and, indeed, in some respects you are. But remember that workers in emotional turmoil probably didn't absorb much until now. So, back to the basics: Where is the organization heading? Why is the organization changing? What will the work priorities be for your team? What are the organization's new core competencies? What are the new job skills and accountabilities?

The potential for innovative and creative ideas will never be higher than now, when the old structure is crumbling and the new exists only in the realm of imagination. To focus creative energy in this chaotic environment, leaders should do the following:

- Offer employees training in creativity and innovative problem solving.
- Urge workers to question every existing workplace rule and regulation.
- Plan events—picnics, after-hours get-togethers, pizza parties—to unify the previously fragmented organization.
- Encourage a workplace atmosphere filled with the fun and joy of creating something new.
- Set short-term goals with immediate payoffs.
- Initiate pilot projects to encourage experimentation.

Commitment

Commitment is the final phase of the change process, when workers emotionally invest themselves in the new organization. When employees are committed to the success of the transformation, it is again reflected in their questions:

"Why didn't we do this five years ago?"
"What are we going to do next?"

Commitment is a time for celebration. To have transformed an enterprise *and* engaged the enthusiasm of the work force is a tribute to leadership and employees. This fact needs to be acknowledged and celebrated throughout the organization.

Commitment is also a time for rewards. Demonstrate the results the organization has achieved by bringing in customers, suppliers, and competitors to talk about benefits from their perspectives. Single out those individuals and teams whose achievements were outstanding, but find ways to thank everybody for their contribution.

Above all, commitment is a time for learning. Leaders who utilize a living-systems model of change help employees realize that (1) discontinuous change is a never-ending, life-enhancing process of leaps to new forms and (2) adaptive behaviors can be learned and incorporated into more effective strategies for the future. The commitment phase offers a unique opportunity for the entire work force to think back through the change and find the strategies, behaviors, and attitudes that were the most effective with this transition to prepare for the next one.

Questionnaire—Strategies to Excel in Changing Times

Employees

- How did you feel initially about the change?
- What helped you get through any negative feelings?
- To whom did you turn for support?
- What did leaders do exceptionally well?

- What do leaders need to improve for next time?
- What personal strategies, attitudes, and work practices served you best?
- What was the final outcome and how did you influence that outcome?
- What did you learn about yourself?
- What do you plan to do differently next time?

  Leaders

- How did you feel initially about the change?
- How did you handle any negative feeling of your own when dealing with employees?
- To whom did you turn for support?
- What management strategies served you best?
- What did you learn about your leadership skills?
- What did you learn about yourself?
- What did you learn about the work force?
- What do you plan to do differently next time?

When you have answered all those questions to your own satisfaction, you will have taken the first step on the road to transforming *yourself* into a first-rate leader of change.

CHAPTER 5

How Can I Take Control If You Keep Holding On?

Fifth Step: Develop the Core of Leadership

"Leadership is the art of motivating ordinary people to achieve extraordinary results in unusual times," I tell my audiences. "We are certainly living in unusual times today. And just as in the past, our times have produced some unusually gifted business leaders who quite obviously thrive on the challenges confronting them."

But how do *you* know what it takes to lead an organization? audiences ask.

Good question. And the answer is, I *don't* know. At least not from personal experience. But neither do the multitude of psychologists, sociologists, and historians who have written volumes on the theoretical nature of the leadership response to challenge. In the end, the only people who really know how it works are the leaders themselves. This chapter is devoted to 10 of those leaders. Ten highly successful men and women who confronted the new business age head on, saw what needed to be done, and said, "Let's get going!"

Paula A. Banks, President, Amoco Foundation, Inc.

As president of the Amoco foundation, Paula Banks is responsible for international philanthropic and community-relations activities for the corporation. She sets strategic direction and manages an annual budget of more than $24 million. Banks joined Amoco in 1966 after serving more than 24 years with Sears in a varied career that included positions such as director of public relations and human resources director.

Walter Blankley, Chairman and Chief Executive Officer, AMETEK, Inc.

AMETEK is a leading global manufacturer of electromechanical products and electronic instruments engineered for niche markets. In 1996 the company achieved record sales of $869 million and record earnings from continuing operations of $51.2 million. Walt Blankley was appointed president and CEO in 1990 and has served as chairman since 1993.

Robert L. Dilenschneider, President and Chief Executive Officer, The Dilenschneider Group

Prior to forming his own public relations firm, Bob Dilenschneider served as president and CEO of Hill and Knowlton, Inc., from 1986 to 1991, where he tripled that firm's revenues to nearly $200 million and delivered more than $30 million in profit. He is the author of several books including the best-selling *Power and Influence.*

Christie Hefner, Chairman and Chief Executive Officer, Playboy Enterprises

Christie Hefner oversees policy, management, and strategy in all areas of Playboy Enterprises. During her tenure, she restructured operations, eliminated unprofitable businesses, and initiated successful international expansion in publishing, entertainment and new media. Hefner helped found the Committee of 200, an international organization of preeminent women business owners and executives.

Karen L. Hendricks, Chairman, President and Chief Executive Officer, Baldwin Piano and Organ Company

Karen Hendricks has been president and CEO of Baldwin since 1994, and in 1997 was named chairman of the board. Baldwin is a 134-year-old public company with U.S. mar-ket leadership in acoustic pianos. Baldwin has five manufacturing plants and 1,550 employs in North America. Hendricks spent most of her career, from 1971 to 1992, at the Procter & Gamble Company in product development and general management.

Horst Schulze, President and Chief Operating Officer, The Ritz-Carlton Hotel Company

Horst Schulze has been president and COO of the Ritz-Carlton Hotel Company since 1988. The organization owns 33 hotels worldwide and employs 14,000 people. In 1992, the Ritz-Carlton won the Malcolm Baldrige National Quality Award—the first and only hospitality organization to win this honor.

Frederick W. Smith, Chairman, President and Chief Executive Officer, Federal Express Corporation

Fred Smith founded Federal Express in 1971. Best known for setting industry standards with its innovative use of technology and service excellence, the company has approximately 119,000 employees in 210 countries throughout the world. In 1990, FedEx became the first company to win the Malcolm Baldrige National Quality Award in the service category, and in 1994 it became the first global express transportation company to receive simultaneous worldwide ISO 9001 certification. Its 1995 revenues were $9.4 billion.

Susan G. Swenson, President and Chief Executive Officer, Cellular One

Sue Swenson is president and CEO of the AT&T Wireless and Air Touch Corporation's joint venture properties in the San

Francisco Bay Area, Kansas City, and Dallas/Fort Worth. She is responsible for three large regional cellular systems covering approximately 9.2 million people.

Steven Wickstrom, Chief Operating Officer, Reell Precision Manufacturing Corporation

Steve Wickstrom is the COO of Reell Precision Manufacturing Corporation, a $14 million company that produces wrap spring clutches and constant torque hinges for foreign and domestic customers. RPM has been the subject of several news articles outlining its innovative business practices and ethical conduct.

Rita P. Wilson, Senior Vice President, Corporate Relations, Allstate Insurance Group

Rita Wilson is senior vice president of corporate relations and a member of the board of directors of Allstate Insurance Company. Allstate is the nation's largest publicly held personal line insurer with more than 20 million customers and 45,000 employees. Wilson received the 1996 Women of Achievement Award from the Anti-Defamation League.

THE CORE OF LEADERSHIP

I deliberately selected these leaders to represent the widest possible range of business activities in America and abroad today. Each of the 10 has his or her own unique corporate responsibilities to carry out. Each has to deal with widely different competitive pressures, customer demands, marketing strategies, stockholder expectations, and work force requirements. Each represents an organization that is affected in specific ways by the new global economy, the information technology revolution, the disappearance of stable currency values worldwide, and the collapse of the old industrial business paradigm as an organizing model for their companies. But all share one thing: an apparently innate set of emotional and intellectual qualities that make up the "Core of Leadership." The components of that core are (1) vision, (2) integrity, (3) trust, (4) vulnerability, (5) values, and (6) motivation. Together they produce what we all instantly recognize as leaders. How they do it is easier to recognize in practice than it is to define in principle. We aren't just talking about special skills or strategies that these people exercise, we're talking about individual character. Like the force of gravity or the lump of uranium in a nuclear generator, the leadership core works invisibly. And like any living system, it sometimes works intuitively and mysteriously. But its positive effects on others can be readily observed, and those observations, in turn, can be put to immediate use by anyone charged with leading fellow employees at any level of an organization.

Leadership as Vision

"The purposiveness of all vital process, the strategy of the genes, and the power of the exploratory drive in animal and man, all seem to indicate that the pull of the future is as real as the pressure of the past."

Arthur Koestler

In contrast to control-minded authority of the past, today's leaders must exercise power through a shared purpose and vision. An organizational vision is not the same as long-range or even strategic planning. Planning is a linear process—progression toward a goal. Vision is more holistic—a sense of direction that combines a good business strategy with a comprehensive organizational purpose that declares its own importance. A vision describes a business as it *could* become over the long term and outlines a feasible way of achieving this goal. To transform an organization, leaders must adopt and communicate a vision of the future that impels people beyond the boundaries and limits of the past.

Leaders who articulate such visions aren't mystics, but broad-based thinkers who are willing to take risks. Visionary leaders don't have to be brilliant, highly innovative, or incredibly charismatic. But they do have to be intently focused on what it is they are trying to achieve. Fred Smith of FedEx put it in these very practical terms: "If there is *any* indication that the leader is not totally committed to achieving the vision, then all the sweet talk in the world will not get people to support it." When I interviewed the other leaders for this chapter, there was universal agreement that vision was crucial to leadership. Here is a sampling of responses:

Schulze: Leaders are the visionaries. They set the vision for the next level of excellence for the organization and its people, they personally commit to it, and then they align employees with that vision by letting people know the motive behind decisions and actions—*why* we do things as we do—and making employees part of the decision-making process in areas that affect them.

Swenson: Leaders need to create a compelling vision about where the organization is going, gain commitment to it, and bring that vision into reality by making the necessary organizational changes. To do this, leaders need to manage the business strategically and give employees confidence that they can lead the organization to that vision.

Wilson: Leaders have a visionary mindset. They create the change they want to see. Leaders need to be like Bill Gates in this regard, he creates new markets. Leaders have the vision to forecast what's next and the passion to reach into the future and seek out new opportunities to push for greater outcomes. It is incredibly important that leaders clearly articulate the vision, and set expectations through the mental pictures they create and the stories they tell.

Hendricks: I see leaders as "visionaries with their feet on the ground." They have to see far beyond what currently is—they can't just be incrementalists—and they must take risks. But the risks can't be "off the wall," they must be balanced, because right after the vision comes the need to create the reality.

An exercise I use with leaders to help them clarify their personal vision begins with imagining themselves five years in the future. Utilizing full-sensory imagery techniques (they realistically imagine that they, the organization, and the world are five years further on) I ask them to respond to several questions.

Vision Exercise

- When you look around your company, what do you see happening? What do you hear? What do you feel?

    A woman who recently left the major consulting firm she worked at for 12 years and started her own company with two clients, three employees, and small offices in an old building in Oakland, California, responded this way:

    As I walk into the lobby of our new offices in San Francisco, the first thing I'm aware of is the energy level. We are so busy—staff is meeting with clients, working on computers, talking on telephones, gathering in small groups to compare war stories and share successes. We have at least 30 new employees here and it is a truly diverse mix of people—ages, ethnic backgrounds, married, singles—and I see a variety of clothing styles from business suits to blue jeans. I'm proud to see the kind of entrepreneurship we have created in the organization. Employees behave as if they own the business. We are very successful and highly profitable.

- What kind of culture does the organization have?

    It is a collaboration of professionals. There is a unity of purpose supported by full communication of basic business information. The culture is open, relaxed, and vibrant.

- What kinds of products or services do you now offer?

    We have expanded beyond consulting services to include a highly successful series of leadership training programs for corporate managers. And we've opened offices in Chicago and New York.

- What is it like to be one of your employees?

Employees love working here. People know their expertise is valued because they can see the direct link between their efforts, corporate profits, and their bonus pay. They feel respected because they're given the freedom to make critical business decisions, and they are energized and excited by the challenges of the future—to be the best change-management consulting firm in the business. They also enjoy working here because we have a philosophy that includes laughter, play, and fun. We support each other and have a good time together.

- What is it like to be a customer?

Customers are constantly delighted by our firm's professionalism, friendliness, and flexibility. They especially appreciate our ability to utilize their own employees in creating and delivering our services, so that success is shared right from the beginning of a project.

- What is it like to be a competitor?

Our competitors are occasionally our clients, our collaborators, and our resources—so we engage in a friendly rivalry which spurs higher levels of performance in all of us.

- What is it like to be a stockholder?

We are a privately held company.

- What effect is your company having on the community? On society? On the environment?

Our company has adopted a community project—a battered-women's shelter—which we support with money and personal time. We also feel that our work benefits society in general because our consulting services result in businesses becoming more profitable while creating a work environment that is more personally fulfilling for employees.

- What effect has your leadership had on the people in your firm?

I have helped talented people discover their strengths, build their abilities, and use those strengths and abilities in ever expanding arenas.

When doing this exercise, I always have participants close their eyes and *see* the future rather than simply discussing future objectives. I know when they have accomplished this task because people begin to describe their visions in very personal and emotional terms, at which point I tell them that holding onto this personal, emotional quality is what makes the vision come alive when they communicate it to others.

Remember, though, sharing your personal vision is only the beginning. Unless you engage employees in the process of crafting the vision, they won't truly own it. When Dick Kleine was the general manager of the Harvester Works at John Deere (he's now vice president of quality) the company adopted lean manufacturing principles—and totally transformed the way combines were made: "We started with a group of 14 employees—about half out of the shop and half from the office—and got them together to write a vision statement about the way we wanted to be. They came up with 10 parts to that aspiration—including communication, trust, job satisfaction, and customer satisfaction. That document became the vision that drove employees toward change."

Leadership as Integrity

A corporate task force at Federal Express identified integrity as a key leadership dimension necessary for successful leaders within FedEx. Leadership integrity is defined as adhering firmly to a code of business ethics and moral values, behaving consistently with corporate values and professional responsibility; not abusing management privileges; gaining and maintaining trust/respect; serving as a consistent role model in support of corporate policies, professional ethics, and corporate culture; and doing what is morally and ethically right.

According to the executives in my sample, a leader must be seen to stand for something, must act from deep-seated principles, and must rely on strong personal beliefs:

Hendricks: The person whose leadership qualities I try hardest to emulate is someone I've known and watched for a long time. John Smale was chairman and CEO of Procter & Gamble for 17 years before he went on to become the chairman of the board at General Motors. I admire John for many reasons: He's a true visionary, he makes bold, leaps-of-faith decisions, and his leadership stands the test of time. Unlike some individuals who head corporations, John is not ego-driven (although he certainly has an internal sense of self-confidence), nor is he particularly charismatic. Instead, he inspires confidence by being what he is—honorable, ethical, admirable, and highly principled. No one ever questioned John's integrity because he was never self-serving. You always knew his motive was to make Procter & Gamble the best.

Wilson: When you ask me what leaders need to *be,* a lot of characteristics come to mind, but one thing is primary: leaders must be highly ethical.

Banks: Leaders must have the highest integrity. Everything leaders do—coaching, mentoring, encouraging risk, helping people grow and develop, creating a sense of urgency, and communicating a *passion* for excellence—must be firmly rooted in integrity.

Dilenschneider: Leaders need to be highly ethical within their own set of guiding principles. That is the key—to be true to a *personal* set of principles. And so, although they may have different principles, both Jesse Jackson and John Walter of AT&T are people of high integrity.

Leading with integrity implies a willingness to embody the attitudes and behaviors you want to see in employees. Gandhi said, "You must become the change you want to see in the world." The leaders I interviewed said much the same thing:

Wickstrom: We need employees to be responsible—which to us means trustworthy and accountable. In our company we try to create relationships that allows us to "call" one another on behavior that doesn't meet this standard. A recent example occurred during the development of our latest strategic plan. Every year we get the top dozen leaders together once a week, for six to eight weeks. At the end of each of the weekly sessions, we have "homework" assignments to prepare for the next meeting. At the beginning of one session, a participant told us that at the last meeting he had offered to send us information which we had agreed to review and return with our comments. He went on to say that of the 12 messages he sent out, he received only 3 responses. He then asked all of us what we were going to do about this issue of "irresponsibility." The meeting stopped and we discussed how to better honor our commitments. Right at the top of the organization's leadership, we are aware of the need to mirror whatever behavior we expect to receive in kind.

Swenson: We need employees to be receptive to being asked tough business questions and not taking it personally. So, in my forums and meetings, I encourage people to ask me tough questions and then I try to respond absolutely candidly, without being defensive.

Schulze: When the Ritz-Carlton opens a new hotel or resort, I personally conduct a seminar for all employees—from general manager to housekeeper. I begin my presentation with these words: "I am president of Ritz-Carlton . . . I am an important person." I pause and then continue, "You are all important people too. You make this hotel run. If I am absent for a day, no one would notice. But you, ladies and gentlemen, would be missed. You make this company the best in the world."

At the Ritz-Carlton, we believe that employees, as well as guests, should be treated with respect and caring. The behavior of leaders should serve as daily examples. Often it is the small things that matter most. If I say that the organization respects and cares about employees, then it is inexcusable for me to pass any employee in the hallway without saying hello.

Leadership as Trust

The essence of business as we move into the twenty-first century is going to be tapping the talent of good people. It's not about how you locate the plants, it's how you locate the best people and motivate them. It's how you trust them and have them trust you.

Reuben Mark,
CEO, Colgate-Palmolive

The chairman of Matsushita Electric Industrial in Japan, Konosuke Matsushita, gave this statement about his assessment of U.S. leadership:

> We are going to win and the industrial West is going to lose. There's nothing much to it, because the reasons for failure are within yourselves. With your bosses doing the thinking while the workers wield the screwdrivers, you're convinced deep down that this is the right way to run a business—getting the ideas out of the heads of the bosses and into the hands of labor.
>
> For us, the core of management is the art of mobilizing and pulling together the intellectual resources of all employees in the service of the firm. We have measured the scope of the technological and economic challenges. We know that the intelligence of a handful of technocrats, however brilliant, is no longer enough. Only by drawing on the combined brain power of all its employees can a firm face up to the turbulence and constraints of today's environment.

If that was a valid criticism of U.S. leadership in the past, it is less true today. In a world of continuous change and fierce global competition, leaders know that what differentiates top companies from the rest of the field is organizational flexibility and the ability to use *everyone's* ideas. Companies that respond to marketplace demands with quick, innovative solutions have a competitive edge.

Until recently, managers' primary function was supervision—telling employees what to do and measuring how well they did it. But the new breed of individualistic employees increasingly don't want or need to be supervised. They need to be set free in the sphere of their own authority. A critical element to leading in new ways that encourage participation and responsibility is a deep belief in the potential of your employees to make responsible decisions. To make responsible decisions, workers need information, support, encouragement, and resources. The amount of information that leaders give the work force is proportional to how much they trust their people. The issue of trust is also pivotal in a living-systems model of organization, where leaders begin with a strong vision or intent—not a set of action plans—and expect plans to emerge locally from responses to the needs and contingencies inherent in that intent. In this model, it is crucial that leaders trust the organization's intelligence to organize in whatever way the future requires.

Trust is an attitude of confidence in another person, a positive set of expectations about that person's competencies and character. The powerful influence of one person's expectation on another's behavior is known as the "Pygmalion Effect." Eliza Doolittle explains it in George Bernard Shaw's play *Pygmalion:* "You see, really and truly, apart from the things anyone can pick up, the difference between a lady and a flower girl is not how she behaves but how she's treated. I shall always be a flower girl to Professor Higgins because he always treats me as a flower girl and always will; but I know I can be a lady to you because you always treat me as a lady and always will." The difference between leaders who complain about the lack of responsibility in today's employees and those who speak with pride of the creative contributions and dedication of their staff may lie in the realm of management's expectation.

Blankley: If you want people to stick their necks out and take responsibility, you've got to provide them with information and training, remove obstacles to performance, and establish boundaries for empowerment that are within people's training and abilities. But first of all—most of all—you've got to trust them.

Banks: Leaders must embrace and live out the reality of empowerment—and that's hard. First, you have to build a qualified, competent, strong team. And then you must allow the members to participate fully in developing plans and goals and bringing those plans and goals to fruition. Even on those occasions when the solution is absolutely clear to you, you have to be careful not to impose your ideas. Difficult as it is, you have to be willing to let go and let the answers come from the team.

Wilson: Not only must leaders model the behaviors they want to see in others, but the modeling must come out of a fundamental, passionate *belief* in people. If you can't trust people and can't relate to them in a holistic way, you miss a fundamental part of what it takes to lead.

Leadership as Vulnerability

When Columbus sailed across the Atlantic, he didn't have a business model.

Intel CEO Andrew Grove
(addressing the Davos economic
forum on how difficult it is to develop
a strategy in fast-changing times)

Recognition of the potential of the work force for contributing solutions to organizational problems has increased while the infallibility of leaders and the certainty of management tasks have declined. The unquestioned authority of leaders in the corporation of the past has been replaced by the need to acknowledge the expertise of those below and to enlist employees as true partners. Moving from a model in which leadership made all the decisions and knew all the answers to an organizational environment of openness, candor, and empowerment takes a willingness by leaders to become and remain highly vulnerable.

There was never a time in which our organizations experienced more uncertainty and chaos. No one can predict the future and no one has all the answers. In this unpredictable business atmosphere, no decisions are permanent, not even the mission or core functions of the organization. Effective leaders don't promise to supply all the answers. Often, more is unknown about the exact direction of the organization than is known—even at the highest levels.

By accepting and sharing imperfections, leaders show they are not afraid to look weak or uninformed in front of others, and that frees other people to admit that they don't have all the answers either. These are confusing times for all of us, especially for those who are trying to make major decisions in a sea of change. No one leader can fully absorb and comprehend the colliding tyrannies of speed, quality, customer satisfaction, foreign competition, diversity, and technology. As GE's Jack Welch put it: "If you're not confused, you don't know what's going on."

Banks: Frank Brawley was the vice president of distribution at Sears. When I think of people who most influenced my career, Frank is at the top of the list. He took time to know and understand me, and he valued my input because he recognized I had abilities beyond my current job title. But I think that Frank's greatest strength as a leader was that he understood what he *wasn't*, and he gathered people around him who could mitigate those shortcomings. As an example, Frank knew he had a "short fuse", so he wanted people who could "call him" on that behavior in ways that were straightforward and yet acceptable in public settings.

Blankley: The best leader I ever encountered wasn't in business. He was my high school basketball coach, Jack McCloskey—who, by the way, went far beyond coaching high school and finally ended up as the general manager of the Detroit Pistons. Jack was the most focused person I ever met. He focused so intently on the goal, he convinced all of us that we could reach it. But it wasn't until he showed an imperfection that we knew the depth of his character.

We had been on a winning streak and then we lost a game that we should have won, and afterward the team was despondent over the defeat. Jack looked at us and said words to this effect: "You might as well save your tears. You should have done something about it on the court where it mattered." The next day before practice, he sat us down and apologized for his behavior: "I'm sorry. I was wrong to have said what I did. I know you really tried. That's all I can ask of you." Our season ended so well that four of us on the team were offered college scholarships.

Wilson: I've been lucky to work with two great leaders. The first was Jack Callahan who was the former President of the Business Insurance Division of Allstate. He had the ability to bring all of himself forward, so that his weaknesses were perceived as real strength. When I interviewed for my first job at Allstate, Jack was an executive vice president. I remember meeting him and thinking, "There just might be a place here for someone like me."

Our current CEO Jerry Choate combines an incredible discipline around the ability to see the total landscape with the abilities to create a vision around that totality and bring the vision to execution. But lately I have noticed that Jerry, like Jack, is the most effective at really *reaching* people when he is the most "human" and vulnerable.

Swenson: When leaders are perceived as human and vulnerable, employees identify with those attributes and begin to see the potential for success and leadership in themselves.

Leadership as Values

We've learned . . . that the soft stuff and the hard stuff are becoming increasingly intertwined. A company's values—what it stands for, what its people believe in—are crucial to its competitive success. Indeed, values drive the business.

Robert Haas, CEO,
Levi Strauss & Company

Webster defines value as "a principle, standard or quality considered inherently worthwhile or desirable." The root is the

Latin *valor*, which means strength. Values are a source of strength for an enterprise or an individual. As leadership strategy moves from coercion to cooperation, the key to bonding people to the goals of the organization automatically becomes the intangibles—relationships, commitments, and shared values.

An organization with cohesive values is like a hologram: Every part contains enough information in condensed form to display the whole. A hologram is a wonderful image for an organization. An observer can see the whole organization's culture and ways of doing business by watching one individual, whether a production floor employee, the receptionist at the front desk, or a senior manager. There is a consistency and predictability to the quality of behavior. The organization achieves this quality through a combination of simply expressed expectations of acceptable behavior and the freedom available to individuals to align their actions with the boundaries of the whole organization's values.

A sales manager read an article about his company's refusal to deal with any country when "under the table" money was part of the negotiation process. He circled the article and wrote the words "Right On!" in the column, and mailed it to his CEO. Like the sales manager, many employees I speak with agree that they are happiest working where the values of their organizations reflect their own. Likewise, the leaders I interviewed were adamant that values played a critically important role in their organizations.

Schulze: Values (the philosophy and practices) are the heart and soul of our organization. The sign outside means nothing if the heart and soul are not in it. It is not enough for people just to fill functions. They have to know what we are all about.

Leaders must stay focused on values and keep them energized—which is the hardest part. For that, you need to find processes that renew and reenergize values. One process that

Ritz-Carlton uses is called the "Line-up." Fifteen minutes before shift begins every day, the leader of the line-up goes through the basics of that day. Employees of Ritz-Carlton all over the world are reminded of the same "value of the day," as prepared by the corporate office. Added to that is a "teaching": an issue brought to our awareness, based on customer-service input, and then some comments about the daily value that are customized to the individual hotel.

The Ritz-Carlton Credo

The Ritz-Carlton is a place where the genuine care and comfort of our guests is our highest mission.

We pledge to provide the finest personal service and facilities for our guests who will always enjoy a warm, relaxed yet refined ambience.

The Ritz-Carlton experience enlivens the senses, instills well-being, and fulfills even the unexpressed wishes and needs of our guests.

Our motto is: We are Ladies and Gentlemen serving Ladies and Gentlemen.

Wickstrom: The three founders of Reell Precision Manufacturing (RPM) shared many basic convictions about the importance of balancing work and family responsibilities and the need to practice ethical principles in the workplace. Our values reflect a willingness to place the well-being of employees and their families above unfettered profit growth, and a commitment to doing what is right even when it doesn't seem profitable, expedient, or conventional.

Reell Precision Manufacturing Corporation

RPM is a team dedicated to the purpose of operating a business based on the practical application of Judeo-Christian values for the mutual benefit of *coworkers and their families, customers, shareholders, suppliers, and community.* We are committed to provide an environment where there is harmony between work and our moral/ethical values and family responsibilities and where everyone is treated justly.

DO WHAT IS RIGHT We are committed to do what is right even when it does not seem to be profitable, expedient, or conventional.

DO OUR BEST In our understanding of excellence we embrace a commitment to continuous improvement in everything we do. It is our commitment to encourage, teach, equip, and free each other to do and become all that we were intended to be.

TREAT OTHERS AS WE WOULD LIKE TO BE TREATED

SEEK INSPIRATIONAL WISDOM by looking outside ourselves, especially with respect to decisions having far-reaching and unpredictable consequences, but we will act only when action is confirmed unanimously by others concerned.

Dilenscheider: Values are very important—*if* they relate to the company. But there is no such thing as a "universal set of values." The catechism of General Electric is not appropriate for General Dynamics or General Foods. Values can't be imposed, they must spring from the experiences employees have in the workplace. The leader's role is to find what those values are and then build a corporate "folk lore" around employee behaviors that exemplify the values. Corporate lore began in one oil company when technology was pretty primitive. People in the oil fields offered wonderful examples of comprehensive analysis and attention to detail, so competence and thoroughness became company values. Now, of course, the company has gone "high tech" and the examples have changed. But the same core values live on—and can be illustrated by a series of stories from the company's history into modern times.

Banks: Values are critical. One of the reasons it was relatively easy for me to make the transition from Sears—where I worked for 24 years—to Amoco was that the values of the two organizations were closely aligned with each other and closely aligned with my own values. This is not to say that at Amoco we always act on our organizational values, but most certainly, the *intent* is present in our daily interactions with customers and with each other.

Amoco Progress

Amoco Progress is our personal and corporate commitment to continuously challenge and improve everything we do to add value for our customers and give Amoco a competitive advantage. We will achieve Progress through:

Customer Focus: Identifying, agreeing on, and then satisfy-ing customer requirements to create value through customer–supplier partnerships.

Business Process Improvement: Ensuring that our business processes—what we do and how we do it—add value in meeting our strategy and the requirements of our customers.

Measurement and Assessment: Using balanced measures, external benchmarks and performance assessment to drive improvement, establish accountability, and build capability.

Leadership: Providing leadership through example. Always challenging ourselves to improve and holding everyone in the organization accountable for rapid and continuous improvement.

Teamwork: Creating an environment that cultivates and rewards teamwork.

Empowerment: Empowering people throughout the organization with the information, skills, and authority to improve their work and holding them accountable for making the improvements.

Sharing Best Practices: Enhancing our capacity to communicate and use our learning and best practices across the
corporation to accelerate improvement of our business results.

Blankley: Values are extremely important. They are most effective—and by effective I mean that people assume them and
use them to guide their behavior—only when the values are
known and when leadership adheres to them. Then values can
be a tremendous force for unleashing the ability of people.

Wilson: There is a moment when a circus performer lets go of
one trapeze and before she grabs the next one in which nothing
is known for certain and she hangs, between trapezes, in
midair. In organizations, "hang time" comes after you acknowledge the contribution of the past to the future. At that point
you must release the past to advance to a future you can't yet
grasp. For an organization to stand solid through this period, it
needs to have solid values.

Allstate's Aspirations:
We Will Be a Great American Company When . . .

We Attract and Retain *Customers* at the Highest Rate in the
Industry, AND . . .

Our Work Processes Are "Best in Class," AND . . .

Our *Employees* Say They Are Personally Fulfilled and Proud
to Work Here, AND . . .

Our *Shareholders* Earn a Superior Return.

Hendricks: I came from Procter & Gamble and I still carry its
values statement in my wallet, so I know that values are *ex-
ceedingly* important. But I also know that values can degener-
ate into empty slogans unless they are reinforced by behavior.
One of my first acts as CEO at Baldwin was to take all the val-

ues statements off the walls because there was no organizational activity to indicate that we were even trying to move in their direction: It was ludicrous for us to say "We value people above all else" when we didn't even have a director of human resources, and it was totally meaningless to talk about "the value of feedback" when some employees hadn't had a performance appraisal in 30 years. What my core management team and I decided to do is to create our own values statement and then work at expressing those values through our action for at least one year before we even talk about values to the rest of the organization.

Smith: Corporate values are the reinforcing mechanism for the achievement of objectives. For example, if our vision is to become the best express company in the world, our values—the way we treat people, the high service standards we set—become reinforcement for reaching that goal.

Federal Express's Corporate Philosophy

From its inception Federal Express has put people first both because it is right to do so and because it is good business as well. Our corporate philosophy is succinctly stated: People–Service–Profit.

Hefner: Values—regardless of whether or not they are formally stated—are important in all organizations. It is foolish for any leader *not* to recognize how much people are influenced by the values of a company's culture.

Playboy's Values

- Stay close to the market
- Create products of the highest quality and value with lead pricing
- Operate with a sense of urgency

- Take ownership for our products and the company
- Decentralize decision making
- Foster a "let's try it" attitude
- Respect the dignity of individuals
- Invest in training; build careers
- Encourage a "have fun" environment

Swenson: We take our values very seriously by making significant attempts to support them not just in formal programs like training and performance management but in our daily interactions with one another. We need to do this in a way that *demonstrates* our values. That is not just an empty phrase—it is how we try to live.

Leadership as Motivation

Technology is so pervasive today that almost any company with enough money can buy any new development it wants. In our industry alone, we are seeing one bank after another introducing new electronic products in a game of technology leapfrog which has left the customer bewildered and confused. Yet the competitive advantage seems to be leaving the realm of technology and entering the realm of the individual. Why? Because only the human being has the capability—the emotion, creativity, and motivation—to bring the benefits of technology to life.

Chris Andersen, Senior Adviser,
Royal Bank of Canada

To be effective motivators, leaders must have insight into the human heart and sensitivity to the hopes and aspirations of others. When the renowned Broadway director and choreographer Bob Fosse died, reporters commented on the immense loyalty his performers always showed him. One dancer summed it up for everyone when she said: "We always knew that whatever Bob asked us to do—even if it was difficult or felt awkward— was to make us look good."

A manager at a utilities company had a similar experience

with a leader in her career: "We knew he wanted us to succeed. He was always acknowledging our good work and, at the same time, always pushing us to improve. He had an almost *magical* ability to urge us to excel in ways that never trivialized our current achievements." Memorable leaders inspire exceptional levels of commitment and performance:

Swenson: The best leader I ever worked for, Lee Cox of Pacific Telesis, combined the ability to understand organizational dynamics with an exceptional ability to deal with people. At meetings he would pose questions that left us curious, energized, and motivated. We couldn't do enough for him. Sometimes I wondered if we were all hypnotized. I've never seen people work so hard for someone and still want to do more.

Dilenschneider: Barney Clarke, the CEO of Columbia Gas Systems, was brilliant—a genius who thought *way* outside the box. Although I suspect he had the answers all the time, he spent hours talking with us, involving us, and making us feel as if we were an integral part of a huge change—as if we were making history. And he got so much out of all of us. We'd work round the clock. Working with Barney was exciting, incredibly intense, and absolutely thrilling.

The secret to being a great motivator is knowing that motivation isn't something that can be forced or ordered. Motivation is an intrinsic capacity of human beings that can be tapped, nurtured, and developed—but never coerced. In essence, all motivation is *self-motivation,* it manifests when leaders hold a compelling vision of the future, have a strong personal desire to realize the vision, and possess the ability to engage people's individual motivation in the common cause of that vision so that a true interconnection emerges.

Wickstrom: People want to know that they are significant and that what they do matters. They want the experience of belonging and being appreciated for their contributions. As a leader, this is an area where you must be careful *not* to be so efficient that you become ineffective. What I mean by that is, if I have 100 employees, it is useless to make a point of saying something appreciative to every one of them every week—even though that strategy looks highly efficient. But it can make a tremendous difference in their motivation if I spend a several minutes with a half dozen workers during the week—showing my genuine appreciation for the job they are doing and reinforcing how that job fits into the bigger picture.

Hendricks: It's not enough to be a visionary. The vision must be shared to the point that it inspires others to pull away from the past and to follow the vision. It's easy to have followers when all the facts are in, but leaders must be able to inspire people to bet on a future that can't be proven and believe in a reward that is yet to be realized.

Smith: Employees must have a minimal level of skills to do a particular job. Leaders must be able to motivate people from the low end of the performance spectrum (doing the least amount possible without getting fired) toward the end of the spectrum where people consistently do the best job possible. One of the best leaders I ever had was my staff sergeant in the Marine Corps. He embodied the characteristics of true leadership and made us want to give our very best *every* day on *every* assignment.

Swenson: Spirit is the natural motivation that is created when people know how what they do makes a difference. That's why it's so important for the individual to be clear about how his or her role fits into the objectives of the organization. Leaders need to motivate people toward the results that drive the business forward. This means engaging people's curiosity so that they ask the right questions, their caring so that they focus on customer-service principles, and their energy—which is why I always say the work and fun are not incongruous. Fun *is* energy.

FROM MANAGEMENT TO LEADERSHIP

Several management experts note that U.S. organizations are overmanaged and underled. If this is an accurate observation, now is the time to correct the imbalance. You might be able to manage stability, but you must have leadership during transitions. Virtually all the leaders I interviewed made clear distinctions between the skills of management and the spirit of leadership.

Dilenschneider: Managers focus on what is happening. Leaders focus on what is *possible.* Managers are process oriented, they make the gears mesh and the trains run on time—and this is important because most leaders can't do it. Leaders inspire people to higher levels of achievement. They generate ownership and pride.

Banks: Managers deal with processes, programs, and projects. Leaders provide people with vision and coaching. They create a sense of teamwork—you work *with* leaders, not *for* them.

Smith: Management is the analytical science of ascertaining what the organization needs to do to become more successful and efficient. Managers utilize quantitative tools and skills. Leadership is the process of coalescing a group of individual activities and efforts toward not just individual but organizational goals. Leaders need to have tremendous personal commitment to the vision and the ability to enlist support from others.

Wilson: In general, management has to do with the here and now—work flow, processes, and resources—and leadership is more future focused and visionary. It requires risk taking, out-of-the-box thinking, and creating a supportive environment in which people can truly develop their potential. I rarely see this as an either/or issue. I think we have to work at being very good at both management and leadership. But there is a point in your career when you have responsibility for other people's success. At this point, you'll need to spend the most time developing your leadership abilities.

Transforming Managers into Leaders

From Manager	To Leader
Uses power to persuade others	Shares power and responsibility
Expected to know the right answer	Initiates search for multiple right answers
Hands-on involvement	Self-directed teams
Gains compliance	Builds commitment
Enforces rules	Presents clear choices
Punishes failure	Encourages and analyzes failure
Takes success for granted	Celebrates and analyzes success
Protects people from negativity	Communicates candidly
Motivates through "pep" talks	Builds climate for self-motivation
Builds dependence	Develops new leaders
Set goals for others	Inspires people to set and reach their own high goals and standards
Controls and commands	Liberates potential
Expects loyalty	Encourages mutual loyalties
Communicates in words	Communicates through congruent words and actions
Process oriented	People oriented
Focus on present task	Focus on future possibilities
Thinks incrementally	Thinks in discontinuous leaps

DEVELOPING FUTURE LEADERS

In today's "knowledge work"—with its reliance on project teams and cross-functional collaboration—leadership in peer relationships is becoming increasingly important. As the guidance of team efforts tends to shift to whomever has the needed information or expertise, more people in the organization must be able to assume the role of leader. More than ever before, successful corporations can't just wait for leaders to emerge, fully developed. They must actively seek out people with leadership potential and find ways to nurture and develop that potential.

Banks: When I interviewed for this job with Amoco, I was asked to describe my leadership style. At the time, we were having lunch on the 40th floor of a building, so I looked out the window and said, "Instinctively I know when a person's wings are ready for them to fly on their own, and I push them off the

40th story, even when they are not yet confident of their own abilities. And their wings flutter and spasm, and then they open and I watch people take off. Of course, the first time I push people, I make sure there is a safety net 25 stories down, and then on the second 'flight' I move the net another five stories down. On the third flight I remove the net."

I look for people with passion and a thirst to continue to grow. Potential leaders are people who don't stop at doing a good job, they always go the step beyond. Another important ability is to be able to see beyond the current problem to connect it with the bigger picture. For example, we might be faced with the business challenge of how to increase the number of our customers. Well, lots of different strategies could be employed to that end. I look for people who grasp the bigger issue—how do we grow brand equity into a household name?—and are able to make the solution to the smaller problem fit as a step in the larger context.

At Amoco, we have specific training programs designed to develop leadership skills. But beyond that, we have groups inside the company—different organizations for women; African Americans; Hispanics; and gay, lesbian, and bisexual employees—that are sponsored and supported by the company.

Blankley: At AMETEK, we have a leadership development team which consists of myself, the COO, the CFO, the head of human resources, the group presidents, and the corporate counsel. We meet for one week during the year to talk about the leadership talent we want to develop within the company—as well as what talent we may need to acquire. Of the 280 people who get stock options, I probably know 275 of them personally.

A few years ago, the leadership team attended a weeklong program at the Center for Creative Leadership and now the company has sent our third group of leaders there. At CCL you go through an extensive psychological and behavior analysis, aided by 360-degree reviews, and then you build your plan for personal development. The problem with any program is that when you return to the real world, it is easy to forget to follow your plan. Our success with the CCL approach is greatly enhanced by using a counselor who comes in once a month and encourages people to focus on what they set out to accomplish.

Dilenschneider: Future leaders need to be mentally prepared for the task of being a leader. This starts with developing an ability to think outside the box by constantly asking "What if . . . ?" and developing plans around a variety of possible scenarios. But the most important mental preparation for leadership is to learn how to keep a sense of perspective through the heights of successes and the depths of failure and setbacks by understanding that in both cases "this too shall pass." Keeping your balance at all times can be extremely difficult because leaders play the game at the highest and lowest levels—they experience the glory of the victories as well as the shock and disappointment that also come with the territory. The trick is not to let the glory go to your head or let the disappointments devastate you. Future leaders are developed by giving people the freedom to succeed and fail, and the guidance to help them deal with both.

Hefner: At Playboy, we empower and encourage people throughout the enterprise to identify those who have leadership potential. Then we offer a leadership development program to acknowledge and develop that potential. Employees who want to be leaders here need to realize that leadership is *not* about having a large number of people reporting to you or even wearing the title of executive. Leaders are the *influencers* in an organization—and any employee's current relationships, interactions, and reputation afford great opportunities to demonstrate leadership abilities.

Schulze: We have a leadership profile taken from our top leaders that we use to identify candidates who have the highest potential for leadership. We are looking for those who have the ability to live in accordance with our values. And, in general, we found that among the most successful leadership qualities are a genuine caring about people and the ability to develop interpersonal relationships.

Smith: We found out long ago that people need to have certain identifiable traits to be effective as leaders in our environment at Federal Express. Our Leadership Evaluation and Awareness Program begins by employees identifying themselves as candidates and expressing a desire for the company to prepare them for management positions. With a recommendation from their managers, these employees participate in a process called "Is Management for Me?," which explains the demands of management as well as the personal characteristics and traits needed for successful leadership. (I find it interesting that once they know the demands and requirements, some 70 percent of the participants drop out of the program.) Those who elect to remain go through a panel and peer review and then enroll in "Management Practices I," which teaches the principles and practices of management and leadership.

Swenson: How one goes about developing future leaders depends on the maturity of the organization. Our company is relatively young and leaders here need to take a hands-on approach to coaching others to leadership roles. They need to be able to teach, to give positive and constructive feedback. And they have to like doing that. We're in the process of creating a 3- to 5-year plan to get the next level of people ready for leadership. We're compiling the results of a "leadership assessment"—a combination of different surveys, profiles, and employee satisfactions ratings—to help determine the basic skills that leaders need to develop. For those with high leadership potential, we create situations where people learn on the job: challenging assignments that rely on success in a team environment, increased opportunities to observe current leaders in action, lateral moves to develop a broader base of the processes of the business, and, of course, lots of coaching.

Wickstrom: At RPM, supervisors are called advisers. Although every employee has only one adviser, the advisers may have as many as three or four "advisees." Beyond the particular functions of their job, advisers take on the role of developing their advisees. In this way, leadership is continually encouraged and developed on a one-on-one basis.

Wilson: Allstate has a succession planning process that goes all through the organization. It begins with our definition of leadership as achieving results *and* creating a supportive environment. To do both things well, we identified 14 critical success factors for leadership. And these factors can be condensed into six key behaviors:

- Be visionary
- Establish high-performance standards for yourself and others
- Communicate, communicate, communicate
- Treat employees with dignity and respect
- Do not compromise the company's goals and values
- Constantly seek new knowledge and learning

Dilenschneider: People need to recognize that there are two paths in life: The first is to be a fine, upstanding person who never pushes himself or herself to play the game at higher levels. And this is a good choice—perhaps a safer choice. But if you believe, as I do, that we are on the earth for a short time and that the purpose of life is to discover our gifts and utilize them to the best of our abilities—and then you *don't* try to play the game, you will never fully realize your potential.

It is unquestionably true. Realizing full potential is the ultimate goal—and not only for leaders. Tapping the maximum potential of the entire work force must be the objective for all enterprises—and enlightened leadership is only half the battle. Most modern businesses, however liberated their corporate philosophies, are still three-dimensional structures with strong vertical components in which the majority of players remain formally subordinate to the people who hire, train, and reward them. For any organization to make real progress toward the fully interactive living-systems model called for in the new business age, it must also rethink its "compact"—the relationship existing between employer and employee. Chapter 6 examines the dilemma of the inherited hierarchical business structure and considers ways to "level the playing field" so that people throughout the organization can start seeing themselves as equal participants in a cause shared by all.

I'll Never Love a Company That Can't Love Me Back

Sixth Step: Renegotiate the Compact between Employer and Employees

THE WAY WE WERE

The fundamental premise of the new model executive . . . is, simply, that the goals of the individual and the goals of the organization will work out to be the same. These young men have no cynicism about "the system," and little skepticism. . . . They have an implicit faith that The Organization will be as interested in making use of their best qualities as they are themselves, and thus, with equanimity, they can entrust the resolution of their destiny to The Organization. . . . the average young man cherishes the idea that his relationship with The Organization is to be for keeps.

William H. Whyte, Jr.,
The Organization Man (1956)

You went to school, you acquired marketable skills, and you got a job. You worked hard, contributing your time and energy to the organization you joined. You made personal sacrifices for your job, some at the expense of your family. In return, your grateful company rewarded you with job security, incremental raises, and promotions based on length of tenure in the "corporate family." And after 30 or 40 years with the organization, you retired with a comfortable pension and the congratulations of your boss and colleagues.

In the "old deal" employer–employee compact just described, workers were guaranteed job security in a safe, stable organization. Factory giants of the industrial age protected their workers by offering fair compensation and lifetime security. Sometimes as part of this social compact, employers provided subsidized housing near the factory site. In the spirit of this paternalistic relationship, Americans referred to their employers by nicknames: Bell Telephone was "Ma Bell," Pillsbury was "Mother Pillsbury," and Kodak was "The Great Yellow Father." And in return for paternalism, employees were expected to be exceptionally loyal. They stayed with one company for the length of their career, followed orders without challenging the status quo, did good work, and supported the positions of their organizations both privately and in public.

THE CHALLENGE OF TRANSITION

The traditional compact between employers and employees no longer exists. Workers cannot expect lifetime employment and instead are responsible for their own career development and job satisfaction. To many employees, it seems as though the balance has tilted in favor of the employer and that the company has abandoned its responsibility to them. People feel they have traded a paternalistic relationship for a one-sided loyalty in which they are expected to work harder than ever in an atmosphere of confusion and impermanence, without having their concerns acknowledged or their efforts adequately rewarded.

When the compact feels heavily weighted to the advantage of employers, the natural tendency of employees is to withdraw their loyalty and commitment. As employment security flies out one window, employee loyalty goes out the other. The paradoxical result is that as organizations strive to reinvigorate work force spirit, employees grow steadily more passive, acting on new directives and directions but without committing to the goals underlying them.

The fact that so many workers have this perception about the current state of their relationship with their employers points to the difficulty we are all having trying to make the transition from the traditional to the new workplace. The rules were changed but not by the companies. They were changed by the new business environment that forces companies to be more accountable, cut costs, and respond with greater speed to ever more volatile markets.

LOYALTY REDEFINED

My concept of loyalty is not "giving time" to some corporate entity and in turn being shielded and protected by it from the world outside. Loyalty is an affinity amongst people who don't expect to be sheltered from an increasingly competitive world; they want to grapple with it and win in it and ask only for fair and respectful treatment if they do not. Their personal values and dreams and ambitions cause them to gravitate toward each other and toward a company like GE that will give them the resources and the opportunity to flourish and win. This is the loyalty that continues to grow, because, unlike a paternal, feudal, fuzzy concept of loyalty, this is an *ongoing, voluntary compact that is continually renewed.*

Jack Welch, CEO,
General Electric Corporation

Loyalty has two dimensions: the internal or emotional level and the external, behavioral aspect. Internally, loyalty is a feeling of bonding, mutuality, affiliation, and caring. Various dictionaries define loyalty as "true, constant, or steadfast in allegiance." One definition is "faithful to a person, ideal, custom, obligation, duty or organization." Another definition is "devoted attachment and affection." For our purposes, the key to defining loyalty starts here: *Loyalty is first of all an emotion that is experienced internally as caring and concern for another person or entity.* Loyalty is basic to our nature as human beings—a potent force that can be brought forth for the good of all.

In his book, *Passions Within Reason: the Strategic Role of Emotions,* Cornell University Professor Robert H. Frank states that emotions are not just the "fuzzy thinking" that most other economists believe them to be. "Rather," he says, "emotions serve a highly useful function. They short-circuit some types of self-interested behavior by bonding people to external projects, to beliefs, and to relationships which are not always in the individual's narrow self-interest. Emotions cause people to feel strongly about things outside themselves."

Because emotions are obviously intangible, it is through the behavioral dimension that we evaluate another's loyalty to us. In organizations we often have expectations of loyal behavior that are implied rather than explicit. The "loyalty compact" was a set of mutual expectations regarding the manifestations of loyalty by both the organization and the work force. In today's organizations, loyalty is manifesting itself in new and sometimes radically different ways. Employers and employees alike need to understand the changing dynamics of organizational loyalty and how to apply that understanding in the workplace to create bonds that will serve them in the future, because it is not only the employer who has developed new definitions of loyalty but the work force too.

In the past, employee loyalty to a company was synonymous with following orders and not questioning authority. In contrast, today's most loyal workers speak up to identify problems and implement improvements. A traditional manager who still equates loyalty with blind obedience may interpret employee criticism as egotism or interference. But the "new style" employer sees active involvement as a positive expression of commitment: "They speak up because they care about what happens to this company."

Loyalty can no longer be equated to length of service, either. Especially in the new Gen-X work force. Flying from Washington, D.C., to San Francisco, I sat next to Laura, a highly regarded human resources specialist in her late 20s. She told me that during an interview for a management position, she was asked a standard interview question: "Where do you see yourself within this company in 10 years?"

"I don't think I made a very good impression," Laura said. "I told them that I didn't see myself staying with *any* company for the next 10 years." Nonetheless, Laura believes she is a loyal employee. According to her: "I always choose to work at a company where I can be loyal to my employer. I show my loyalty by working hard, being extremely dedicated and honest, and by contributing far beyond my job description. It's just that I'm more interested in developing my abilities than I am staying with one organization forever."

LOYALTY AND RESTRUCTURING

Frank was a loyal employee at a Fortune 500 company, a man on the "fast track" according to his envious peers. When the company began restructuring, Frank's career stalled. He was moved from a line-management position into a staff function and was finally assigned to an organizational task force. Feeling that his talents weren't being utilized, Frank's morale plummeted: "I never thought I'd feel this way. I used to come to work 'all fired up.' Now I simply put in my time. How am I supposed to care about what happens to the company when it doesn't care about me?" Six months later, Frank left to join another firm.

As sure as Frank's experience destroyed his sense of loyalty, Samantha's loyalty was actually strengthened during a downsizing: "Last year we found that our entire department was going to be eliminated. At a time of corporatewide cutbacks, my boss helped all of us relocate to other jobs within the company. She really went to bat for us. She set up interviews with different department heads, checked later for feedback on how well we did, and once I even heard her on the telephone saying, 'Well, could you try him anyway? He doesn't make a very good first impression but I promise you he can do the job.' Believe me, I am very loyal to this organization."

THE KEY IS MUTUALITY

In progressive organizations across the country, a new kind of relationship grounded in mutual trust and respect is emerging between employers and employees. This new compact is developed out of realistic expectations on both sides. It is a path that reflects the new paradigm for business and society in a global market as it attempts to align the interests of the organization with those of its employees, to share both the risks and rewards of doing business.

As leaner companies rely on fewer employees to shoulder more of the work, the developing relationship between company and worker is changing from paternalism to partnership: Companies owe it to their work force to aggressively pursue new ideas, products, services, markets, and customers. Employees expect to be treated fairly, to develop professionally, and to have meaningful, challenging work. In return, employees owe the organization their willingness to participate in business growth, idea development, customer service, and organizational transformation. Balancing the employee–employer compact is not a matter of adding more items to one side of the balance sheet or eliminating some from the other side. Increasingly, it is a matter of finding items that are of value to *both* the employer and the employee. Robert Haas, the CEO of Levi Strauss says, "We are at the center of a seamless web of mutual responsibility and collaboration . . . a seamless partnership, with interrelationships and mutual commitments."

The University of Western Ontario developed a strategic plan with mutuality in mind. The plan concluded with these words: "We must also acknowledge and deal with the fact that inviting uncertainty, the risk of occasional failure, and a certain amount of dislocation demand that we respect the loyalty to self that a staff member must have. The institution cannot expect an individual to make great sacrifices at personal expense. We will not succeed unless we create an environment in which personal and institutional goals are reinforcing."

CREATING THE NEW COMPACT

Like many other companies, Kodak was looking for ways to change from an entitlement-based culture to a performance-based culture. Unlike many companies, Kodak utilized world-wide sessions with all levels of Kodak people to develop the priorities for a culture that would drive and support a sustainable strategy for long-term business success. Kodak established key values—respect, integrity, trust, credibility, continuous improvement, and personal renewal—as a fundamental part of the new relationship. The rest was created by employee focus groups throughout the company. According to Michael Morley, the head of human resources: "The result may not be what an English teacher or an ad agency would have produced, but it represents what people actually said to us."

GROWING A PERFORMANCE-BASED CULTURE AT KODAK

As a Company We Will Provide

- Clearly defined corporate goals and vision
- Rewards based on performance against clearly defined objectives
- Market-competitive salary, bonuses, and benefits
- Opportunities for growth
- Competent leadership at all levels
- Open, honest, two-way communication
- Actions consistent with the corporate "talk"
- A developmental, learning environment
- Respect for individuals and honest behavior

(continues)

- The resources to get the job done
- Flexibility in dealing with career, personal, family, and cultural differences

As Employees We Will Provide

- 100% effort with a positive attitude
- Good business decisions and accountability for our behaviors
- A motivated, dependable work force
- Continuous improvement of our skills and competencies
- Creative, innovative ideas to better serve customers
- The initiative to understand the business and Kodak's customers
- A Kodak team working for the good of Kodak, the team, and individuals
- The results we promise
- Dedication to company success
- A willingness to accept change
- Pride and a sense of ownership in the company; "ambassador" of the company

Royal Bank of Canada took a 93-person cross-section of its work force off site for a weeklong conference to create the basis for Workplace 2000—a vision for the changing employee–employer relationship. The group drafted this outline of the new understanding to be presented to all employees:

> If you buy into the organization's values and goals, contribute energy and ideas, grow and develop personally, and take care of our customers then together we will create a good work environment, provide all the challenge you can handle, help you develop new skills and broaden your experience, and offer support and guidance for career and professional growth. And, you'll be a part of a company setting the pace in its industry; you will enjoy working here, manage the pressure, and see how the pieces fit together.

PARTNERSHIPS FOR AN EMERGING WORKPLACE 2000

Royal Bank Group provides

Training, learning, development opportunities
Rewards, recognition, pay for your contribution
Challenging job and growth opportunities
Technology support
Support for employability, marketability
Support for personal and family needs
Professional HR support

Employee provides

Commitment to work, teamwork, and customer
Work skills in keeping with changing jobs
Contribution focused on business objectives
Personal ownership of development and growth
Flexibility
Effective people management
Attitude

Allstate never set out to create a document about the changing employee–employer partnership. The organization had just rolled out its program on diversity education, and the diversity team was given the task of creating the next phase—how to keep renewing the organization's commitment to diversity. A team member came up with the idea of crafting a formalized statement of mutual commitments between employees and employer. And that idea initiated a process of discussions with leaders and key employees in both informal one-on-one settings and structured focus-group sessions. The document that was created as a result of this participation follows.

THE ALLSTATE PARTNERSHIP

Allstate expects you to:

1. Perform at levels that significantly increase our ability to outperform the competition
2. Take on assignments critical to meeting business objectives
3. Continually develop needed skills
4. Willingly listen to and act on feedback
5. Demonstrate a high level of commitment to achieving company goals
6. Exhibit no bias in interactions with colleagues and customers
7. Behave consistently with Allstate's ethical standards
8. Take personal responsibility for each transaction with our customers and for fostering their trust
9. Continually improve processes to address customers' needs

You should expect Allstate to:

1. Offer work that is meaningful and challenging
2. Promote an environment that encourages open and constructive dialogue
3. Recognize you for your accomplishments
4. Provide competitive pay and rewards based on your performance
5. Advise you on your performance through regular feedback
6. Create learning opportunities through education and job assignments
7. Support you in defining career goals
8. Provide you with information and resources to perform successfully
9. Promote an environment that is inclusive and free from bias
10. Foster dignity and respect in all interactions
11. Establish an environment that promotes a balance of work and personal life

CUSTOMIZING THE NEW COMPACT

In sales, knowing that there is no universal "sales pitch" is crucial to success, as the following story illustrates: An insurance salesman stuck his head into a sale's manager's office door and said, "You probably don't want to buy any insurance, do you?"

"Young man, whoever taught you to sell? You never say, 'You don't want to buy insurance, do you?' " The sales manager continued to lecture the young man on salesmanship, stressing that every customer's needs are different. "What you lack is confidence. I'll buy some of your insurance to build your confidence."

After the appropriate papers were signed, the sales manager said, "Now remember what I told you. Every customer is different. You must use a different approach for each customer." "Oh, I do that already," said the salesman. "This is my approach for sales managers, and it works almost every time."

Forward-thinking organizations know that there is no universal approach to defining the new employer–employee relationship. Every company needs to collaborate with its workers to find the mutually beneficial arrangement appropriate to that enterprise. Following is a guide for creating the new employer–employee compact in your organization.

Query the Work Force

Distribute a questionnaire to the entire work force and gather employees' answers to the following questions, then communicate the results to the entire organization. (An interesting and often insightful exercise is to have employees fill out the questionnaire first, then have senior managers fill it out the way they *think* employees have responded and compare the responses.)

- How do you define workplace loyalty/commitment?
- On a scale of 1 to 10, how important is it for you person-

ally to feel loyal to the organization you work for? (Why is
this a high or low priority for you?)

- How do you show that you are loyal to your organization?
  (What work behaviors, attitudes, and other actions
  demonstrate your commitment?)

- On a scale of 1 to 10, how important do you think it is for
  the organization to have a loyal/committed work force?
  (Why?)

- How does management already show that it is loyal or
  committed to you? (What policies, strategies, benefits, behaviors, attitudes, etc., demonstrate its commitment?)

- What would you specifically *want* management to do to
  demonstrate commitment/loyalty? (What policies, strategies, benefits, behaviors, attitudes do you want most from
  management?)

- Does being loyal to the organization conflict with any
  other of the important commitments in your life? (Does it
  conflict with your commitment to yourself, your family,
  the customer, the community, your values, etc.? And, if it
  does, how does it conflict?)

Create a Forum for Discussion and Interaction

Include the entire company or use a task force composed of a
cross-section of management and employees. The purpose of
the forum is to explore the kinds of employer–employee relationships that are evolving in today's leading organizations. Use
the information you gathered from the questionnaires as a way
to stimulate a candid discussion. Then address these specifics:

- What was the traditional workplace compact between this
  organization and its employees? (What did employees expect when they first joined the company? What did they
  think the company expected from them?)

- What part(s) of the old relationship will remain viable for the organization and its work force in a changing business environment? (Is there any part of the "old deal" that will work in the future?)

- How are other organizations approaching this issue? (Use my examples, illustrated earlier in this chapter, of Kodak, the Royal Bank of Canada, and Allstate—or from other companies that developed a viable new compact between employers and employees.)
- What does *this* organization need most from its employees and what can it realistically offer?
- What do *our* employees want from the organization and what are they willing to give?
- Based on the new reality of a constantly changing business environment and workplace, what kind of relationship is mutually beneficial to management and workers? (What's our "new deal?")

THE COMPACT IN ACTION

After interviewing thousands of employees and after being involved with the "compact negotiation" process in several organizations, I find some of the same employee needs and demands coming up again and again. Although your organization may be unique, the following areas are becoming part of what I call a "culture for commitment" in many companies:

- Open and honest communication
- Professional development
- Equity and fairness
- Employee participation
- Work-life balance
- Recognition and appreciation

As you read through the rest of this chapter, take note of what other organizations are doing in these areas and use them as "benchmarks" for your own corporate culture.

Honest Communication

Open and honest communication means sharing knowledge—
especially in challenging times. Although some organizations
find it difficult to let employees in on the details of negative
decisions, Reell Precision Manufacturing (a producer of mechanical wrap spring clutches for precision applications) com-
municates candidly to employees about what they can expect
from the organization during a downturn in business. When
new employees join RPM, they receive a guidance manual
which, among other things, defines RPM's philosophy of employment security. The manual states:

> When short-term imbalances occur in our workplace, we
> could follow the example of some other companies and quickly
> lay people off or encourage people to leave. We do not think
> that is a wise choice. In the history of RPM we never laid any-
> one off or let anyone go due to a short-term change in business
> conditions. There were times when we found it necessary to
> freeze pay or even reduce pay to protect our long-term future.
> When this happens, we all share the burden. We are committed
> to providing secure employment and a stable income for all
> regular coworkers as long as the corporation can at least break
> even. In the event that payroll reductions are necessary, we'll
> share the available work and pay rather than expect any of our
> regular coworkers to be deprived of employment. If conditions
> ever deteriorate to the point where we cannot break even,
> even by payroll reductions, we will seek input from all other
> coworkers before the triad (the senior leadership group) de-
> termines an effective response.

Last year, this policy was put to the test. In the autumn of
1995, RPM's sales forecasts for the following year were $14 mil-
lion. In January, though, that projection suddenly fell to $11
million when a key customer greatly reduced its order. In line
with RPM's stated philosophy, workers were first asked to reduce nonpayroll expenses. The results were substantial but not
sufficient to cover the shortfall, so RPM held a companywide
meeting at which employees were given a 30-day notice before

implementing an across-the-board pay reduction of 10 percent. At that meeting, employees were given a complete account of the process senior management went through in weighing options before arriving at their decision. At the end of the meeting, the employee audience spontaneously applauded. Five months later, loyalty remained high, profits were back up again, and salaries were restored.

Why was the salary cutback at RPM so successful? Here are the answers according to Steve Wickstrom, the COO:

> We have *wired* the organization in an open and honest way. Employees didn't make the decision, but they knew *how* we did and *why* we did. One of the benefits of letting the work force in on the entire process is that it exposes people to the complexity of the situation, they get to see the struggle we go through, and they really understand that there are no easy answers. We succeeded because we gave employees candid and thorough information.

Professional Development

The growing awareness of the mutual importance of training to employees and employers can be seen in corporate programs across the United States. One example is Intel's Corporate Staffing Program—a strategic redeployment process that allows talented employees to move quickly from one business within the organization to another. This is part of Intel's new employee compact that holds workers accountable for their continued employability and holds the company accountable for informing and training workers so they will *be* employable. Intel informs employees about which businesses are declining and which are emerging, so that people have adequate time to plan for their redeployment. Intel utilizes information systems to provide employees with direct access to job opportunities and skill requirements and provides them with resources to assess their existing competencies, identify knowledge gaps, hone skills, deepen training, or even retrain completely.

Another example is the Work Force Development Program (WDP) at USAA. USAA is a worldwide insurance and diversified financial services association headquartered in San Antonio, Texas. *Fortune* magazine named it the most admired property and casualty insurance company in the country in its March 3, 1997, issue. When many companies find themselves with a work force that no longer has the skills needed to do their jobs, they fire those employees and hire new ones with the requisite skills. At USAA, management has made a commitment to provide reskilling opportunities to all employees. As a direct response to the issue of worker employability, the WDP was created with the goal of providing employees the necessary information and resources for self-assessment, tailored education, training, and skills enhancement to prepare them for current and future jobs. Going beyond a traditional approach to skills building, the WDP helps employees understand what USAA believes it will need in 5 to 10 years in terms of skills and human resources and how to improve their chances of staying employable. Although career assessments and counseling have been available at USAA for many years, this new program helps focus available programs and resources. Centers companywide help employees to obtain information about opportunities within USAA, receive one-on-one guidance on enhancing their employability, and gain access to a wide variety of resources. The program is designed to help employees discover what they aspire to and how those aspirations can be tailored to fit the USAA of tomorrow.

The Equity Factor

As companies downsize, restructure, and refocus, employees are asked to do more and work harder. And they have, on the whole. But many feel angry and disappointed that they have not been rewarded for their increased productivity, and their anger is most frequently apparent in their reaction to executive compensation. Big disparities in pay between executives and the work force—especially in times of downsizing and plant closures—can damage employee loyalty.

Recently I talked with an employee who was having second thoughts about her commitment to her company. "I've been with this organization for over 15 years," she told me.

> I've always loved my job and felt like an important part of the company—as though we were all in this together. I've enjoyed the good times and always understood when salaries or benefits had to be reduced during the hard times. I used to be a "gung-ho" employee. Well, last month I read that our CEO is one of the highest paid executives in the world; I also know that we just had a very profitable year. But in spite of that, we're being asked to take cuts in our health care and other benefits. For the first time, I'm wondering if my loyalty has been misplaced.

The issue is not just monetary compensation but equity across the board. To energize a work force, it is going to be increasingly important that companies develop equitable relationships that reflect a true partnership. Many companies are now redesigning compensation plans in response, aiming specifically at giving employees a real stake in the future of the company.

At the mini-mill steel manufacturer Nucor, every employee's pay depends on the steelmaker's profitability. Steelworkers at Nucor are eligible for productivity and quality bonuses of 130–150% above their base pay. This averages out to about $50,000 per year—about the same as unionized workers earn at other mills—but because of the new plan, productivity at Nucor has risen enormously. Less than one worker-hour is needed to produce a ton of flat-rolled steel, as opposed to four worker-hours elsewhere.

Share the Credit for Success

Be generous when handing out credit for an accomplishment. A television director who was employed by CBS for more than 25 years told me: "There are two ways you can 'pull' a performance from a cast and crew. One is to intimidate them. The other is to put your ego aside and make everyone as big a part of the overall success as possible. I've tried both ways. The second works better."

Share the Profits

When Intel, the world's largest microchip maker posted a net income of $1.9 billion fourth-quarter earnings in 1996, its revenue reached $6.4 billion for the year—up from $4.6 billion in 1995. To celebrate, the company announced a $1,000 bonus for each of its 48,500 workers—totaling $48.5 million.

S. C. Johnson Wax turns profit sharing into an annual celebration. This privately held company, which has provided profit sharing to its employees since 1917, distributes an initial payment to workers in June. Then, in December, the year-end check distribution becomes a major event. All headquarters-based employees (about 3,000) are invited to attend an elaborate holiday party, business update, and employee-recognition ceremony—and to receive their bonus checks. The program concludes at about noon, and that marks the official end of the workday as well as the beginning of the corporatewide Christmas/New Year's holiday. The festivity, excitement, and spirit of camaraderie end the year with exactly the kind of spirit that Johnson Wax is famous for engendering in its employees.

Give and Get Objective Performance Appraisals

It is crucial for the development of employees that they have accurate and clear feedback about their talents as well as those areas in which they need to improve. It is equally important for leaders to get objective feedback from workers on what *they* do very well and not so well. Federal Express, Kraft, State Farm Insurance, TRW, Merck, and Levi Strauss & Co., are just a few of the successful organizations that augment traditional management performance appraisals with 360-degree performance appraisals.

Look at Retention from an Equitable Perspective

According to current Department of Labor statistics, today's new employee will, on average, have 8 to 10 jobs and as many as 3 or 4 different careers during his or her lifetime. Work force retention is not loyalty—it is only one manifestation of loyalty. As I noted earlier, any one of a variety of forces may dictate that an individual (or a function or an entire department) no longer serves the goals of the organization. Employees need to understand this reality and accept that there are other ways for employers to display commitment beyond a promise of ongoing employment. A similar new understanding must be accepted by employers. There are many forces (life-style choices, family obligations, personal development, etc.) that may influence a *loyal* employee to leave an organization. Sue Swenson of Cellular One tells employees that she *expects* them to leave the company if they are offered a better opportunity elsewhere.

Don't Ask Others to Do Anything You Wouldn't Do Yourself

When the Chevron plant in Richmond, California, wanted to mandate arbitrary drug testing for employees, all senior managers submitted to the testing for a full year before asking employees to do likewise. As a leader, by displaying ethical behavior and setting high personal standards, you demonstrate a willingness to observe the same set of standards and performance criteria that you require from others.

Communicate Equity through Actions

The best way to communicate your concern for equity is with behavior, not rhetoric. Several years ago I interviewed Sam Walton, the founder of Wal-Mart. He told me how he and his top managers went about building a sense of equity and partnership with 215,000 employees—many of them unskilled workers with starting pay of less than $5 an hour. The company began with an organizationwide campaign entitled "We Care," and everyone at Wal-Mart became an "associate." But Walton didn't stop with just a corporate communications program—Wal-Mart was also one of the first organizations to give hourly associates, as well as their department heads, access to figures regarding costs, freight charges, and profit margins. And when a store exceeded the profit goal the company set, the hourly associates shared part of the additional profit.

Bank of America wants employees to feel and act like owners, so the company initiated its "Take Ownership" plan—one of the largest stock option awards programs ever devised—granting more than 85,000 employees (including part-time and hourly workers) the right to purchase between 350 and 540 shares each over the next three years.

As a check against unfair or arbitrary exercise of power,

Federal Express, CitiCorp, and Borg-Warner Company are among the 100 companies that use peer review boards to help resolve employee grievances. An unbiased appeal process proves to employees that their company stands behind its commitment to equity in all situations.

Increase Sensitivity to Areas
That Might Be Perceived as Inequitable

A close look at the psychology of relationships reveals that most individuals attempt to keep a mental balance between what they contribute to a relationship and what they get back from it. When employees believe that they are putting more into their company than they are getting back, or when they do not perceive the rewards distribution to be equitable, commitment slips dramatically. As employees look for balance through equitable treatment, it is their *perception* of an event, rather than the event itself, that defines reality.

I interviewed employees at a public utility where workers were negotiating a 2 percent raise and management was resisting the cost increase. At that same time, the fleet of corporate vans was repainted. Instead of viewing this as a necessary expense, the employees' perception was that it was unfair of the company to spend money on vehicles while it argued about a salary increase with employees: "How dare they throw money at those trucks and then quibble about a lousy 2 percent raise!" The retired CEO of a chemical manufacturing company put it this way: "Commitment is fragile. It is built or destroyed daily. As a leader, you must make it a routine part of your decision-making process to ask the question: Will this action be *perceived* as equitable by others?"

Value Diversity

Valuing differences—having a deep appreciation for what makes people unique—is not only an important issue for employees, it is critical to any business that needs to serve a demanding customer base in a global marketplace. Organizations that make a commitment to diversity demonstrate that commitment by their efforts to attract diverse job candidates, offer diversity education, create minority networks, and celebrate diverse holidays. But the best companies don't stop there. They go beyond just tolerating differences and work to build a culture of respect, which views diversity as the fuel for creative energy and insight.

Headquartered in San Francisco, Just Desserts is a wholesale and retail baker with $14 million gross revenue. The company has been named "best bakery" by Bay Area publications for the past 20 years. Its 320 employees include immigrants from all nationalities, gay couples, and former felons. At Just Desserts, everyone's beliefs and values are accepted and people are encouraged to be themselves. Employees are evaluated on two things: doing their job and getting along with fellow workers. "You can't find the best, most creative solutions unless people are free to be who they are," says the CEO, Elliott Hoffman. "If employees are uncomfortable, anxious, or angry, they shut down and don't do their best work."

The desire to create an inclusive environment, where everyone feels valued and where everyone is able to contribute, is quickly permeating the most successful organizations in the United States. The following is excerpted from a 1996 letter to Marriott managers from the lodging director of diversity:

> Each Marriott manager will play a leadership role in making diversity a part of our corporate culture. This will require us to look beyond mere compliance with the law; we must begin to see diversity as an *asset to our business* and *encourage the special talents and diverse perspectives* of each associate to

produce quality service of superior value for all of our customers. Diversity should not be referred to as a fad, project or program, because *diversity is a long-term commitment* to organizational change.

Understand the Equity Issue of Executive Compensation

Netscape Communications CEO Jim Barksdale will accept only $1 in salary this year. In a document filed with the Securities and Exchange Commission, Netscape said that Barksdale will forgo his salary and bonus because he "believes that his compensation should be linked to the long-term interests of the company's stockholders."

Barksdale's decision comes at a time when executive pay in the United States is going through the roof and when executive compensation is a hot topic of conversation for employees around the water cooler. But, in the eyes of the work force, the issue is not simply high salaries. (Employees know that bosses make money—that's one reason workers aspire to join the upper ranks of management.) The real issue, again, is equity. The enormous salaries, lavish stock options, and golden parachutes offered to executives give them a vastly greater stake in improved financial performance and much less downside risk than the rest of the work force experiences. The declining trust in top management that employees express among themselves reflects the belief inside most companies that, regardless of corporate rhetoric, we are *not* all in this together.

Conversely, Barksdale's decision was seen as a gesture to rally morale at Netscape, the Internet company whose shares have fallen on hard times. The stock, which peaked at $85.50 in December 1995, hit a 52-week low of $25 a few days before Barksdale's announcement. Netscape workers closely follow the stock because they all have stock options, which give them the right to buy shares at a preset price. When the share price drops, the value of the options drops as well. Barksdale's decision to waive his salary is seen by employees as an expression of his belief in his ability to increase the value of the stock significantly in the near future—at which time everyone will benefit.

Employee Participation

Empowerment, employee involvement, participation, and broadening individual responsibility are all ways to describe a workplace trend that gives employees control over decisions affecting them. Employees today are seeking more freedom of choice and more authority. And companies that empower employees in this way are already reaping the benefits.

At the Ritz-Carlton, employees are empowered as teams to solve problems that directly affect them. Here's how it works: If a particular hotel has as its primary customer complaint a problem with room service taking too long, the manager would inform employees in that department and ask for volunteers to form a committee to find the root of the problem in the room service system and to change or create a different process that solves the problem. By the same token, if two different departments have a conflict—say waiters are dissatisfied with dishwashers because the banquet service isn't ready on time—members of both departments form a cross-functional team (as internal customer and supplier) to find the process problem and solve it. According to the president, Horst Schulze, "Employees are finding the cause of the defect and eliminating it rather than correcting it temporarily." In addition to this approach to teamwork, individuals on the staff are empowered to make decisions to please or appease a customer— even when it costs the company up to $2,000—without having to check with any supervisor.

Participation is not just a "nice" thing to do for employees, it is a financially sound business strategy. An MIT study comparing automotive plants with similar technology found that plants with innovative work practices—including extensive training, work teams, pay for performance, and participative management—manufactured vehicles in an average of 22 hours with 0.5 defects per vehicle, whereas traditional plants took 30 hours with 0.8 defects per vehicle.

Work-Life Balance

At a business meeting on the East Coast, I met an executive who handed me his business card as an introduction. I was startled when he abruptly snatched it back. He explained that he wanted to cross out the word *senior* in front of his vice president title. He went on to tell me that he was only temporarily acting in the senior position and that, as soon as possible, he wanted to return to his old job. He said that five years earlier his ambition was to be president of the company, but not anymore: "Being a vice president suits me just fine. I'm good at it, and I could do it in my sleep. I don't need the added pressure of a higher position. Besides, I have a family and a couple of interesting hobbies. This gives me time to 'play' with them."

Increasingly, people are looking to balance a variety of interests and commitments. They are not as likely to think, as do some of their bosses, that the world begins and ends with the office or factory. I've heard this sentiment expressed in a variety of ways:

> "I love my job, but it's not my whole life."
> "If the company ever relocated, I wouldn't move. I like my lifestyle here too much."
> "My parents weren't there for me when I was growing up. I will never let a job get between me and my family."

Blending career and family life first came to corporate attention with the influx of female employees after about 1980. Then companies began to find that so-called female issues actually jumped gender lines.

Because more women were joining DuPont's ranks (women made up 28% of the work force by 1986), the company's affirmative action committee decided to survey employees about their child-care needs. They found that child care was not just a women's issue; it was a mainstream employment issue affecting both men and women. Those findings had significant implications for DuPont's ability to retain good staff; a subsequent study found that half of the women and a quarter of the men working at the company had considered moving to a company that offered more job flexibility.

Based on these survey findings, DuPont executives began a process of developing "work-life programs" to help employees deal with issues such as child care and elder care and to balance the demands of work and home. A 1995 survey of employees found that 52 percent of those who took advantage of the programs said they would "go the extra mile" for DuPont, compared to 36 percent of those who did not use the programs.

Other organizations are expanding their efforts at helping employees balance the work-life seesaw: Marriott International renamed its *work-family* unit the *work-life* department and recently added a telephone hotline to give employees advice on life problems ranging from child care, elder care, debt management, and home remodeling to getting a mortgage and buying a car; Xerox offers employees as much as $2,000 a year up to a lifetime amount of $10,000 for such expenses as day care or care for an aged or unwell parent. Employees also receive the $2,000 when they buy a first home, and last year I worked with a company whose reengineering efforts were centered around the key question: *What gets in the way of your doing a good job and having a life?*

At the heart of all these programs is a basic philosophy that takes into consideration the importance of employees' lives beyond the workplace. But no leader articulates this philosophy better or more concisely than Bob Wahlstedt Sr., one of the co-founders of Reell Precision Manufacturing: "If there is a conflict between the job and the family, we expect the employee to resolve the matter in favor of the family."

Recognition and Appreciation

Finding appropriate and effective ways of recognizing employee contributions to the organization remains a difficult challenge for management, but it is one that must be met if companies want to cultivate the emotional attachment required of the work force today. The leadership of some companies has already risen to the challenge.

At Reell Precision Manufacturing, everyone has equal access to special treatment. When any employee has a "policy conflict," he or she writes a short report with the answers to three questions: What's the policy? What would I like to do differently? Why would I like to do it? Then the employee gets the signature of his or her direct supervisor and one of the four company officers. A recent example involved a factory worker. The previous year RPM changed its work hours during the summer months to a different schedule, and the next year the plant was too busy and so management decided not to change hours of operation. However, based on the previous year's decision, one employee had already reset her day-care schedule. She asked for (and was granted) a three-week policy exception to work different hours until she could arrange for the necessary readjustment. A small thing perhaps, but so is the fact that all workers get business cards (without titles) so the person on the factory floor knows that he or she is recognized formally as a valuable, contributing member of the organization. This also means that every employee has a card to hand to the banker when applying for a loan or to give out at social functions. At RPM the small things add up.

When employees today speak of recognition and appreciation, they're talking about an ongoing acknowledgement of their contribution to the organization. Workers are looking for respect, trust, and personal attention. Organizations can validate these needs in several ways.

Make Sure All Appreciation Is Genuine and Heartfelt

If you don't mean it, don't do it. Gone are the days when an annual "gesture" of recognition—the company picnic or awards dinner—can compensate for callous treatment by management during the rest of the year. One unhappy employee put it this way: "How stupid do they think we are? Do they really believe that a lousy chicken dinner is going to make up for treating us like robots?"

On the other hand, leaders who really care about their employees build powerful bonds of commitment. Jim Nordstrom, the former CEO of Nordstrom, told me: "It's no great trick getting people to be loyal. People will be almost *embarrassingly* loyal to anyone who genuinely cares about them."

Include Spontaneous Recognition

Don't make all rewards so predictable or systematic that they become a version of "if it's Tuesday, it must be Recognition Day." Nothing loses meaning faster than the scramble to designate an "employee of month" *every* month. In contrast to recognition programs that are stilted by their predictability, spontaneous, on-the-spot awards immediately acknowledge positive behaviors. Most leading companies are using some form of spontaneous recognition: The Bravo Zulu (Navy talk for "well done") program at Federal Express gives managers the prerogative of awarding a dinner, theater tickets, or cash to any employee who is "caught" doing an outstanding job. And Wells Fargo Bank gave this concept an innovative twist when 16,000 employees were each given awards of $35 to present to a coworker. This peer-to-peer recognition had two distinct advantages: First, the employees knew better than their bosses who actually deserved a special acknowledgement, and second, for each $35 spent, *two* people felt great!

Show Appreciation by Following the "Platinum Rule"

The Platinum Rule states: "Do unto others as *they* would have you do unto to them." As leaders respond to the changing needs, values, and perceptions of subordinates and staff, more companies are dumping old-fashioned award certificates and are bestowing career-boosting privileges on their best workers, such as a chance to increase their visibility, responsibility, or authority. Examples of such opportunities can include time with the boss over dinner or lunch, trips to other locations for special training, meeting important customers, participating in strategic planning sessions, making presentations to senior management, or representing the company at professional gatherings. And remember, one of the most meaningful recognition "strategies" is still a simple and sincere "thank you," given one-on-one from boss to employee.

Give People Personalized Recognition

Employees are individuals who are motivated in different ways. By staying sensitive to people's uniqueness, leaders can tailor recognition to recipients. A boss I know acknowledged the extra time and effort put in by her team with one set of letters of gratitude sent to the employees and another to their families. Sending personal letters to employees' homes might not be appropriate in all cases, but in this situation the leader knew her staff well and she understood the difficulties that the overtime demands created for their families. The result was that her team felt doubly rewarded.

At another company, the boss has each member of his staff fill out a personal profile of hobbies, favorite sports, and preferences for leisure activities. Then, when the boss wants to reward a staff member, he goes through the employee's profile and produces tickets for the ballet, a round of golf, dinner out, etc.—whatever reflects the employee's personal interests.

And if you're dealing with a lot of employees, keep notes. One or two personal details remembered at appropriate moments make everyone feel special.

Treat People with Courtesy and Respect

Trust, respect, and consistency in relationships have always been important to business success. These traits, however, take on added significance today. To show your appreciation for their contribution to the organization, give people your full attention: Listen to them, encourage their questions, support their ambitions, and respond to their ideas with careful consideration. Walt Blankley, the CEO of AMETEK, puts it this way: "A leader is first of all a communicator. But one of the most important parts of communication is listening. And you must really listen, not just use techniques, like repeating what the person has just said, so that you *appear* to listen. I mean displaying genuine respect. I talk with people on the shop floor, and they're too smart to be taken in by some phony technique. They know if it's real." Another CEO's secret to relating exceptionally well with his work force is to "remember that employees are not just talented professionals but also valuable human beings."

Show People How Their Efforts Make a Difference

Most people desperately want to do more than just bring home a paycheck; they want to *believe in* their work. They want to contribute in meaningful ways, and then they want their contributions to be appreciated by the organization they work for. When Ford Motor Company created the Taurus automobile, the company took a prototype on tour to the various parts suppliers. By doing this, Ford showed exactly how those suppliers' products contributed to the value of the finished product. The response was overwhelming. Employees from each company wrote unsolicited letters pledging to continue their best efforts on behalf of Ford.

Reward People Financially for Their Contribution to Corporate Success

No company can be consistently successful without the commitment, enthusiasm, and, oh yes, the *self-interest* of employees throughout the organization. With this very basic understanding of human nature, companies are using the power of financial incentives to revitalize the work force. But few are doing it with as much flair as Levi Strauss & Company. If Levi Strauss reaches cumulative cash flow of $7.6 billion by the end of the fiscal year 2001, each of its 37,500 employees in 60 countries, regardless of position, will get a full year's pay as a bonus. If the company meets its financial goal, it will pay out about $750 million in bonuses to its 12,000 domestic employees and 25,500 overseas employees. Robert Haas, CEO of Levi Strauss, insists: "This transaction does not signal new, more strenuous demands. It says we're all in this together." Most employees interviewed by the *San Francisco Chronicle* on the day of the announcement said they had confidence that their employer would not set a goal that was unattainable. Merchandise coordinator Maria Bernales said, "I think they'll make the goal. They do look after you here."

WHAT THE WORK FORCE GAINS

In an environment of mutual commitment, employees expect honest communication from management, challenging and empowering work responsibilities, recognition and appreciation for their efforts, personal/professional development opportunities, and equitable treatment. In addition to these tangible benefits, employees want to commit to companies because doing so satisfies a powerful, and basic, human need to *connect with* and *contribute to* something significant. "The life committed to nothing larger than itself is a meager life indeed," writes Martin Seligman in his book *Learned Optimism.* "Human beings require a context of meaning and hope."

The findings of an ongoing study by the Stanford Research Institute (SRI) on the changing values of workers offers this corroborating evidence regarding the vital role of emotion in business. SRI is tracking the fastest-growing segment of the work force—"inner-directed" employees—who care about elevating the quality of life, who want their work to make a difference, and who desperately want to be part of something that matters. Individualistic and independent, today's talented "gold collar" workers (as SRI has dubbed them) also want to work for enterprises where they can commit to the goals and identify with the values of the organization.

To inner-directed employees, emotions are a real and essential part of doing business. They value and trust their feelings. Inner-directed workers are seeking a quality of work life that includes deeply personal satisfactions: They want to love their work and bond emotionally with their organization. The strong desire of employees to care about their organizations was something that my own research found again and again. In the hundreds of interviews I've conducted, I never heard a single worker declare: "My career goal is to do mediocre work at a company I hate." Commitment and loyalty are part of who we are as human beings and how we want to relate to our work. Here is a small sample of employee comments from my interviews:

> "I've always had to work where I could be loyal to the company."
>
> "Given the choice between a higher salary and a job I loved, I'd choose the job."
>
> "Commitment and relationship are all there is."
>
> "The difference between a job and a 'calling' is the passion I feel about the work and the emotional attachment I have to the organization."

Peter Senge of MIT's Sloan School sums it up this way: "A corporation can't save your soul, but it can stand in for the age-old idea of people collectively pursuing a path that has real meaning to them."

THE BENEFITS OF EMPLOYEE LOYALTY TO THE ORGANIZATION

Organizations need employee loyalty; that is, they need the caring and emotional attachment of dedicated workers. When employees are committed to their work and to the goals of the organization, employers can expect to see the following results:

- Attract a greater number of talented employees
- Increase employee retention

- Increase employee effort and motivation
- Increase customer loyalty
- Increase corporate profitability

Attract Talented People

Pilots who hold barbecues to thank mechanics, flight attendants who sing safety instructions on board, Halloween-costume contests, and Herb Kelleher's own brand of joke cracking—is that any way to run a business? At Southwest Airlines it is. For the past 25 years, the airline has been envied for its steady growth and profitability. Last year, 137,000 job seekers applied for 5,000 jobs openings at Southwest. And it wasn't top dollar that drew them; pay is about the same as at other airlines. Prospective employees flocked to Southwest because of the company's reputation for employee friendliness and fun.

Increase Employee Retention

The new social compact is short term. Employees now carry their skills with them from one company to another, and many workers consider job hopping a normal route to professional success. Ultimately, of course, it is the best professionals who have most options to go elsewhere and give their ideas and commitment to other organizations.

Companies have always understood that customers are volunteers. They need to understand that, increasingly, employees are volunteers too. Talented workers have options. If an organization wants to become the employer of choice for the best and brightest, it must develop the kind of work environment that attracts and retains top talent.

At Starbucks Corporation, which provides all employees—even part-time store clerks—with health insurance, stock options, training, and career counseling, staff turnover is less than

60 percent annually, well below the 300 percent restaurant industry average.

Chik-fil-A is an Atlanta, Georgia-based fast-food chain that operates more than 600 restaurants nationally. At Chik-fil-A the selection of managers isn't based on experience in the restaurant business but on the answer to one question: *Would I want my son or daughter to work for this person?* The turnover rate among Chik-fil-A store operators is 4 percent to 6 percent annually. The industry average is 10 times higher.

Increase Employee Effort and Motivation

A recent survey by Yankelovich showed that 25 percent of U.S. workers believe they could accomplish at least 50 percent *more* on the job each day. On average, employed Americans say they could increase their output by 26 percent. In our post-industrial world it is not capital assets that will determine the success of an organization but, rather, the intensity of motivation of its employees to continually change and improve to meet or set the next standard. Employees who are emotionally involved with the organization are far more productive than those who have emotionally withdrawn. Companies need employees who are enlightened and willing to participate in a vital, competitive business environment. When I ask employees how they show commitment and loyalty, the response I hear most often is that they are willing to increase their efforts—to "go the extra mile."

Increase Customer Loyalty

In one way or another, we are all in the service business; we rely on customer loyalty for profits, not just for market share. Research done at Harvard Business School estimates that a 5 percent increase in customer loyalty can produce profit increases between 25 percent and 85 percent. Loyalty is a direct result of consistent customer satisfaction. Customer satisfaction is a direct result of the treatment received in those "moments of truth" every time customers interact with employees. And the relationship between the employee and customer is almost always a reflection of the relationship between employee and the organization. Maintaining customer loyalty is impossible without loyal employees who are committed to the service goals of the organization and are willing to extend their best efforts to make sure that customers come back time and time again.

Leo Burnett Advertising has been treating employees and customers as its most valuable assets since 1935. The company invests heavily in recruiting and training, pays new employees well above industry norm, and generally contributes the maximum to pension and savings plans. Burnett possesses the highest employee *and* the highest client retention rates in the industry.

Increase Corporate Profitability

The research results are in. It pays to be nice to employees. A 1993 survey of 700 publicly owned firms from all major sectors found that companies utilizing more innovative human resource practices showed higher annual shareholder returns from 1986 to 1991, as well as higher gross return on capital. The most "progressive" 25 percent of these firms had an 11 percent rate of return on capital, more than twice that of the others surveyed. Firms listed in *The 100 Best Companies to Work for in America* in 1993 had a higher total return (the sum of stock price appreciation and dividends paid) over the previous eight years than did the 3,000 largest companies in the United States. The difference was a substantial 19.5 percent for the 100 best companies compared to 12 percent for the others.

A company's ability to foster employee morale and loyalty is attracting rapidly growing scrutiny in some quarters of Wall

Street. Ernst & Young's Center for Business Innovation presented a study to the Council of Institutional Investors which
showed that investor decisions are 35 percent driven by nonfi-
nancial factors. One "people factor," a company's ability to attract and retain talented employees, ranks fifth among 39 such
factors investors use in picking stocks—right behind strategy
execution, management credibility, quality of strategy, and in-
novativeness.

Even when it is difficult to put a price on it, leaders know intuitively that employee commitment is immensely valuable.
The president of a high-tech company in the Silicon Valley
summed up the opinions of many leaders I've interviewed: "If
given the choice between working with a group of people who
are highly skilled but have low loyalty, and one with average
skills and high loyalty, I'd pick the loyal group because I know
that somehow they'd make it happen."

Over the past several years, I have been a guest on many
radio call-in programs. I especially remember one radio show in
the Northwest, when an unusual number of disgruntled employees were phoning in with corporate "horror stories." People
complained about being unappreciated, underpaid, and misun-
derstood. They spoke of callous treatment from uncaring
bosses and reported that they worked for organizations "just interested in making a buck." For the entire hour, all calls followed the same line. Finally, in genuine disgust, the interviewer
said to me: "The principles you're giving us sound so simple,
why aren't more companies following them?"

I didn't have to think about my reply: "With all the diet books
on the market, why aren't we all thin and trim? What could be
simpler than reducing calories and increasing exercise?" The
answer to my question and his is the same. Things that are simple are not necessarily easy.

As a consultant and speaker, I work with executives and
managers around the world, and not once have I encountered a
boss who despised all employees. On the contrary, the leaders I

meet are good and concerned people. And even if an employer's only goal *were* to increase profits, the evidence is still conclusive that the best way to do it is to empower, to loyalize, and to attend to the well-being of talented employees.

What could be more simple? And what could be more difficult to accomplish?

What amazes me sometimes is that so many of you do it so well.

7

This Isn't the Company I Joined . . . It's Better

Seventh Step: Liberate Work Force Potential

To succeed in an increasingly competitive world, where all organizations strive to *do more with less*, liberating work force potential becomes the key issue.

Carol Kinsey Goman

"Powers or resources not yet developed" is the dictionary definition of potential. Applied to physics, it means latent energy waiting to be used. Applied to a work force it means untapped talents, ideas, and contributive strengths waiting to be switched on. "No company," I always emphasize at the end of my conferences, "uses more than a fraction of its work force's total potential. The companies that do best today are the ones that find means to use a larger fraction than their competitors. *That* is their edge in the new global economy."

But how do they *get* that edge? is the question my audiences always ask.

By taking action, I tell them, based on two fundamental principles:

- Eliminate obstacles to creative collaboration throughout the organization.
- Rely on human potential as central to your corporate strategy.

But how do we know that's right for *our* company?

There are two answers: because I've seen what other companies have accomplished when they applied those principles, and because blocked energy, whatever its source, has the same negative effect on large groups of people that it has on individuals. It narrows horizons, inhibits productive thinking, and creates fear.

I already mentioned my experience in private practice with people who could not adapt to change. The other problem I saw more and more frequently in those days was a deepening anxiety about performance—the kind of "floating anxiety" that blocks action and stifles initiative because of the fear that whatever one does will be wrong. The experience wasn't new; "Rat Race Syndrome" had been around since the 1950s. But I began to notice something different about these particular cases. With increasing frequency they seemed to be rooted in a specific sense of emotional alienation. Men and women who were confident, effective professionals in the familiar surroundings of the old industrial-age businesses world seemed suddenly to find themselves paralyzed by uncertainty regarding their capabilities, their roles, and, in some instances, even their hold on reality in the new post-industrial environment. And, as so often happens when self-doubt strikes in settings where confident behavior is expected, my clients turned their fears in on themselves, went on pretending to perform as before, and eventually ended up in my office. None of these people were suffering from mental illness, nor had any of them lost their ability to recognize reality. But reality was changing, faster than my clients could take it in, and the result was that they simply became so disoriented and fearful that they didn't know how to evaluate the best action to take.

My work with those individuals taught me something about group dynamics that has stood me in good stead as a "corporate therapist" ever since. When anxiety of any kind is blocking effective performance, talking about it is just as helpful with large numbers of people as it is in one-to-one counseling. It may sound ironic, but the corporate leader who can say to his or her employees, "Sure, I'm scared too," will do more for company morale with that single admission than a dozen phony pep talks ever could. Why? Because the open sharing of fears (as well as hopes) creates a sense of genuine community in an organization and a sense of genuine value in each of its members. From that combination comes the sense of belonging that engenders mutual trust, self-confidence, and responsibility, and from those come the transformation of potential into kinetic human energy.

"How you get the process going is up to you," I tell my audiences. "No two companies are alike. No two work forces are temperamentally the same. All I can do is assure you that a lot of untapped potential is there in your work force, waiting to be liberated—and then tell you some success stories about how companies are tapping into that potential."

THE J. D. STEERING AXLE COMPANY: how Jeff Garbin helped to sharpen the competitive edge at John Deere by bringing 15 people closer together

The problem at Deere was declining cost efficiency resulting from too much non-value-added activity in the manufacturing process, so Deere's leadership adopted the principles of "lean manufacturing" and came up with a new idea about factory-floor organization. As part of that restructuring, Deere asked Jeff Garbin to introduce the change-over in one of its departments. It was Garbin's first assignment, and the first thing he did when he became the module leader (shop supervisor) of Department 947 of the John Deere Harvester Works was to ask his 15 employees to invent a name for themselves. Thus, the

Steering Axle Company was born with its corporate slogan: "A quality product built by quality people."

Deere's idea was to abandon the long-standing "cell concept" of manufacturing in which employees merely performed one or two operations on a component before passing it on to the next cell and create instead a "modular production system" in which all employees working on a given component would share equal responsibility for the finished product. Once up and running, the newly formed modules would be treated as independent, in-house minicompanies—with their own corporate philosophies and standards—whose "business" it was to supply John Deere with top-grade, competitively priced parts for assembly into the machines and equipment it sold to the public.

Along with the other new module leaders, it was Jeff Garbin's job to help his employees through the transition. And, as "CEO" of the newly formed Steering Axle Company, he set as his own first goal, "the creation of an environment where people have a mutual sense of responsibility for producing defect-free parts." Eighteen months later, these were the results: a 55 percent reduction in inventory, a material reduction of 7 percent, a direct labor reduction of 12 percent, an overhead reduction of 22 percent, and a lead-time reduction of a whopping 80 percent—from 15 to 3 days. "The key to our success," Garbin explained, "was that workers took ownership and took pride and satisfaction in their jobs. My role was to facilitate that transition through empowerment backed by training and support."

Thanks to Garbin and the other "CEOs" at John Deere, the module system of manufacturing and assembly became the standard factory-floor model throughout the Harvester Works, and soon all of Deere's plants will be organized in the same way—a collection of autonomous, self-managed minicompanies, each wholly responsible for the quality and salability of the component part it produces.

How did Garbin make this model work so well in the beginning? First, he eliminated "human barriers" in the collaborative process that were creating divisiveness among his workers.

> We had 10 people working the early shift and 5 on the late shift. There were people on the two shifts who had never spoken to one another before. They didn't know each other, they came from different manufacturing disciplines, and they had a reputation for not getting along. I began by getting both shifts together in a room for a couple of hours, with no limits on what they were to discuss, except that it *couldn't* be business related. Within three months, people started coming in early or staying late just so that they could talk with people on the other shift about what was happening at work.

The other thing Garbin did, as part of Deere's plan, was to bring his employees physically closer together so that each worker, whatever his task on the steering axle, was doing his job within inhaling distance of his business partners. The different tasks were still carried out individually, as in the cell system, but instead of being scattered all over the factory floor the cells were now pulled together into a single organic whole that could exchange information and share ideas whenever the need arose. As one welder put it, "My customer is about 15 feet away from me. If there's a problem we work it out right then and there. Before, I made these parts and then they went to another corner of the plant. I didn't even know the guys that took them on from me. We should have done this 20 years ago."

In the end, the collaborative obstacle Jeff Garbin eliminated was much more basic than factory-floor inefficiency or employee indifference to John Deere's costing problems. He eliminated isolation. Through module 947 he turned 15 strangers into a group of friends and business associates who proved more than able to make *their* new minicompany a resounding success.

- Look closely at how your workers are relating to one another personally. Don't tolerate divisiveness, resentment, disrespect, grudge holding, or mutual suspicion among departments or individuals. Creative collaboration cannot take place in an atmosphere of animosity. Get your people together however you can. It doesn't have to be work related. Form a stock market investment club, or a poetry society, or a softball team, or a birdwatching group—anything that will let your people know one another better as individuals. And don't hold back because you think you're intruding. How your workers get along *is* your business.

• When a company undertakes any major structural change, the employees affected will join in the process much more enthusiastically if they understand clearly why the change is necessary and what it is meant to accomplish. Don't be mysterious. Give your workers the details, encourage feedback, take action based on constructive suggestions, and don't assume you know more than they do just because you're the boss. Probably the most compelling lesson learned from the John Deere experience was voiced by that welder: "We should have done this 20 years ago."

• Forming independent minicompanies may not solve *your* organization's problems, but there will always be other ways to create closer cooperation and greater responsibility in the front-line work force. Identify the obstacles first, then plan how best to remove them. Then let the workers discuss your plan among themselves and come back to you with their own ideas. I've said this before, but it's worth repeating here: A more empowered work force is a more contributive work force. Forget being a manager, and start thinking of yourself as a leader.

RETHINKING LIFE AND WORK AT XEROX: how the Xerox Corporation created a more contributive work force by paying less attention to rules and more attention to employees' needs

The problem at Xerox's southern customer administration

center (SCAC) was management overefficiency. Xerox had long been renowned as a family-friendly organization. But when the Ford Foundation launched a study into the idea that family-friendly practices can also help improve business results, its researchers discovered a glitch in the works: Managers at the SCAC were so strict about office work schedules that the predominantly female staff of 400 were being forced to use more and more of their personal days and sick time to deal with routine family matters. The managers weren't unsympathetic to the workers' personal responsibilities, and an array of work-family benefits had been in place for years. But lack of flexibility in the face of an increasingly complex and demanding outside world was creating a worker-unfriendly environment without anybody realizing it or talking about it. Managers feared that if they granted more flexible working hours, productivity would decline. Workers fearing management disapproval if they asked for greater freedom were creating the "family time" they needed by other means. As a result, unplanned absences at the SCAC were increasing, phone stations were being left unattended, customers were being inadequately served, growing work force frustration was leading to an accelerated staff turnover—all of it bad for business and all of it in the name of presumed efficiency. When the researchers found similar problems at the Dallas sales/service office and the engineering unit in Webster, New York, they went back to Xerox with a novel suggestion: Why not take scheduling out of the managers' hands and let the employees deal with it themselves? The workers know what their jobs require. They also know what their lives are throwing at them. Let them sort out their own working arrangements—less rigid hours, compressed workweeks, mutually agreed "quiet times," greater freedom to come and go as required—whatever will help to make life and work coexist more harmoniously. These are responsible adults after all. They like the company. They're good at their jobs. The work will still get done.

Xerox agreed to try it, told management at the three centers being studied to hand work schedules over to their employees, and sat back to see what would happen. What happened is that the work forces accepted the challenge gladly, formed self-managed task forces from among their own ranks, and immediately began looking for new approaches to flexible working hours that would take everyone's need into account. The results were striking: At the SCAC, employee morale soared, staff turnover immediately declined, customers began reporting dramatically improved service, and the rate of absenteeism dropped 30 percent. In the Dallas office, sales revenues actually exceeded projections for the year as cross-functional teams made up of front-line sales, service, and support people began addressing not just their department's working hours but questions of work—family conflicts in general, hiring practices, and even staff evaluation methods. And when the office color business team at Webster engineering was given greater autonomy over its work schedule, team members amazed everyone by launching the new Xerox 4700 color printer on schedule—an almost unheard-of event in an industry notorious for last-minute setbacks and delayed product launches.

The success of the Ford Foundation's "people power" experiment was so impressive that this year Xerox plans to launch a companywide initiative to create general use of self-managed employee teams in all areas of the business. "Rethinking life and work" has now become a major strategy in determining how work gets done at Xerox.

- If work force attitudes and behavior are becoming counterproductive, look first at management practices. Nine times out of ten, that is where you will find the obstacle to productivity.
- Even if the work force isn't complaining openly, long-standing company rules in a rapidly changing environment can

produce hidden resentments. Review the rules regularly and talk about them with the people they apply to.

- Encourage front-line employees to discuss all workplace problems candidly and without fear of punishment. The obstacles they're confronting every day may be ones you never even thought of.

- Look for ways to give employees greater decision-making authority over the material circumstances of their working lives. Nothing stifles collaborative initiative like the sense of resignation that comes from feeling powerless. Nothing encourages it more than letting people know they are trusted.

THE GREAT GAME OF BUSINESS: how Jack Stack broke down the information barrier at International Harvester by treating employees like business partners

When Jack Stack arrived at International Harvester's factory in Springfield, Missouri, the engine remanufacturing plant was losing $2 million a year on revenues of $26 million. Stack and the 119 employees of the now independent Springfield Remanufacturing Corporation (SRC) initiated an amazing turnaround. Ten years after he bought the company, SRC had sales of $73 million and the firm hired almost 600 additional workers. How did he do that? By making information available. Stack created a system called "the Great Game of Business," which was designed to teach every employee about the entire business—including the finances of the company. The goal was to give people inside the organization as much information as companies give shareholders every quarter. Each Wednesday employees got a complete analysis of the entire company: income statement, balance sheet, and cash flow for the month. As workers came to understand the entire picture, they also learned how their jobs fit into the whole. So successful was Stack's "Great Game of Business" that SRC now schools other corporations in the rules of the game.

Information is the nutrient of all living systems. In any organization, how information is handled determines whether it is an obstacle to or a liberator of creative collaboration. In traditional management structures, restricting access to information or doling it out on a need-to-know basis decreases employees' power. At SRC, information is used to include and empower the work force. The incredible turnaround at SRC could not have happened without Jack Stack involving every worker through increased access to information—and then investing heavily in the education and personal development of employees so that they would have enough basic background to utilize the business data he shared.

Jack Stack started his corporate transformation with small steps. When he first took over management of the International Harvester division, his primary goal was to increase productivity. Each day he gave foremen the results of how well their people did the day before—how many units they had produced and what percentage of those units contained defects. He also gave them productivity scores for their particular department compared with the other departments within the plant as a whole, so that all five foremen knew how they stood individually and as a group. The first time the division broke its previous productivity record, Stack gathered the foremen and bought them a round of coffee and let them take time to talk, laugh, and feel good about their accomplishment. The second time they broke the record, he bought coffee *and* donuts. The third time, he invited the foremen to his house for pizza and poker.

- Think of yourself and your work force as equally intelligent partners in a war of ideas against the competition. Knowledge coupled with trust triggers inspiration. Give your employees all the information you can and trust they'll come up with the answers you need.
- When large-scale change is required in an organization, cushion the impact by breaking the process down into individ-

ual steps that everyone can understand and deal with. Celebrate each small victory along the way. Be generous with congratulations, but don't be patronizing about it. Your work force isn't made up of good boys and girls. It's made up of thoughtful, aware men and women. They know the difference between being taken for a ride and being invited on board.

REVITALIZING THE "HP WAY": how Lewis Platt reenergized the work force at Hewlett Packard by updating its corporate values

When Lewis Platt became CEO of Hewlett Packard (HP) in 1993, employees were complaining that the 40-year-old "HP Way" was no longer relevant to the company's needs or aims. Some felt that the corporation's famous philosophy became meaningless when Bill Hewlett and David Packard (its creators) retired from the organization. Others believed that its core values, however sound they might remain, simply weren't flexible enough to cope with the problems and uncertainties being thrown at the company by the new global economy. Everyone agreed that unifying values were necessary and that the old HP Way was the key factor in HP's past growth and success. But younger employees, especially, felt that updating was urgently needed to revitalize flagging spirits at all levels of the organization, and during the past four years Lewis Platt devoted an immense amount of effort to accomplishing that aim.

The HP Way is a set of five organizational values that define what is expected of HP employees and what employees can expect in return from the company.

THE HP WAY

- We have trust and respect for individuals.
- We focus on a high level of achievement and contribution.
- We conduct our business with uncompromising integrity.
- We achieve our common objectives through teamwork.
- We encourage flexibility and innovation.

The HP objectives were initially published in 1957. In the original version a short paragraph followed each value statement, explaining how it was to be lived out in six critical areas of organizational behavior: corporate profit, customer relationships, fields of interest (technologies and competencies),continuous organizational growth, corporate expectations of employees, and management responsibilities. In Platt's revision, the language of the objectives and the organizational framework on which they are built was largely unchanged, but the explanation of how the values translate into behavior was updated to reflect the current business and social environment:

- More emphasis on creating an inclusive work environment that values and benefits from diversity at all levels
- More emphasis on injury prevention, product safety, product stewardship, and environmental protection
- More references to suppliers, channel partners, and other business associates, who are a vital part of the HP value chain
- Updated references to HP's growing breadth of product and service offerings, business interest, customer sets, and creative opportunities
- Updated language on employee development, work/life challenges, continuous learning, and career self-reliance
- Stronger, more precise statements of managers' leadership responsibilities

- A direct reference to return on assets as a key measure of HP's success
  - A new paragraph on global presence and competition
  - New language on balancing the needs of our individual businesses with the interests of HP as a whole
  - Stronger language on HP's corporate citizenship responsibilities

Like all successful companies, HP wants to become the employer of choice in its industry. It wants to attract the brightest people (especially new college graduates) from around the world and then earn their loyalty, enthusiasm, and commitment. Lewis Platt believes that the most attractive thing to potential employees about HP's culture is its upfront assumption that people want to do a good job, a creative job, and will do so if given the right environment.

In his efforts to make HP the best place to work, Lewis Platt set goals related to HP employees in four areas: managing work-life demands, diversity, employee development, and maintaining an injury-free work environment. Platt talks about these goals every time he meets with an HP audience, and he continually speaks to HP people around the world in large and small groups. Moreover, Platt follows up his talk with actions: HP now runs a corporatewide diversity training program (in which Platt and the management staff participated first). The company's personnel emphasis moved from recruiting to retaining and promoting, and HP's new policies make it easier to work flexible hours and take leaves of absences. Now at HP, every business unit is asked to identify work–family issues and to propose an action plan as part of its annual business review. So, for example, when HP's printer group had to find ways to increase the number of shifts its manufacturing employees worked, it simultaneously investigated alternatives for round-the-clock child care.

At HP, the result of Platt's efforts can be seen in the company's ongoing survey of employee attitudes, which shows a noticeable improvement in scores over the past four years—especially in employees' higher rating of management. Today, in a comparison with other high-tech companies, HP gets significantly higher organizational-rating scores overall.

• Just like company rules, company values are not immutable. Times change, people change, social and workplace needs change. Review corporate philosophy on a regular basis. Talk to people about their attitudes toward its precepts. Get their ideas about shortcomings and possible improvements. Remember that the liberation of work force potential depends just as crucially on the spiritual environment in which people work as it does on material and economic factors. If work force energy and commitment are flagging, it may well be because long-standing corporate values no longer conform to current realities.

• Apply the concept of continuous improvement to corporate values. Keep constant watch on corporate values in their relationship to global economic changes. What energized a company's vision a year ago may be stifling it today. Think of the revitalization of corporate philosophy as an ongoing process no different from the introduction of new technologies or the recruitment of new talent.

• Remember that the bottom-line aim of any corporate culture is not to *get* more from people but to create an environment in which people want willingly to *give* more.

HARNESSING THE COMPETITIVE SPIRIT: how Motorola uses self-organizing quality teams to liberate the contributive potential of the entire work force.

The cameras, the spotlights, the judges' eyes—all are focused on the diminutive woman standing on the stage. Dressed in a conservative yet elegant cream-colored suit, she stands square to the audience, feet firmly planted. But her upper body is alive, and a broad smile seems to take in all 300 people watching. In rapid-fire fashion, the woman explains how she and her nine teammates saved Motorola $250,000 last year. How they developed and implemented a strategy that increased production and reduced cycle time without additional equipment or labor expense. They did it through empowerment and self-direction.

So begins the June 1994 cover story in *Successful Meetings* magazine. What the reporter was writing about is a program that began in 1988 and is still one of the most highly motivating and inspirational events at Motorola today. People throughout the company form total customer satisfaction (TCS) teams during the course of the year to address problems of quality improvement, production efficiency, profitability, and product innovation. Some team members devote as many as 400 hours a year of their personal time to working on a team's project. Teams meet regularly during the workweek, and most supplement that participation with after-hours and weekend gatherings. TCS teams within the same discipline compete with other teams to find the most innovative solutions to problems, and the winning finalists gather from all over the world for an annual one-day championship meeting at which each team tells its story. Winning the international competition carries no monetary reward. But all Motorola employees look on being a part of the competition as both an opportunity and a privilege—a chance to grow personally and professionally, to initiate the process of identifying and solving problems, and to be recognized by the highest level of Motorola management. It is now widely accepted throughout Motorola that there is no single process for driving change that is as *significant* as the TCS team competition.

No one states the effects of the TCS team competition for liberating employee potential better than the participants themselves. The woman on the stage ended her presentation by thanking Motorola's leadership for "trusting us and giving us the opportunity to realize that we are more than just operators and technicians on the line." In fact, it is the corporation that should and does give thanks to people like that TCS member. Motorola estimates that it saves some $2.2 billion annually from quality programs of this kind, and the company funds the TCS projects without bothering to track the costs because the benefits are so obvious.

The fact is, people in companies have always self-organized one way or another. Regardless of the formal corporate structure, individuals always seek out colleagues they perceive as having the knowledge, creativity, or influence needed to get the job done. What's different at organizations like Motorola is that the company is introducing policies that deliberately free employees to self-organize and get the job done without central planning or control. At Motorola worldwide, thousands of people with complementary skills gather in teams each day under the TCS umbrella. The competition encourages everyone from the kid in the mail room to the design engineer to the patent lawyer to identify problems and collectively find solutions that improve quality and customer satisfaction. According to a veteran Motorola employee: "We are not rigidly structured. We're a 'first-name' company that breaks down barriers. In the early years, management had to encourage teams to form. Now, it's more common for teams to *form themselves.*"

Employee training at Motorola goes beyond the mere technical aspects of doing a job; the corporate mission of total customer satisfaction is build into every training program too. Every employee, every secretary and janitor, is required to take a minimum of 40 hours per year of training. Motorola University (Motorola's education center) offers classes on team building, rotating leadership, and learning how to handle difficult people. There are problem-solving classes, quality classes, classes on human resource psychology, and individual evaluation. Together, these skills form the basis of team building. They are what make the TCS competitions so successful. And the competitions, in turn, are a vital part of what makes Motorola the phenomenal international success it is today. In an very real sense, the competition is Motorola's own greatest success story.

At the inception of the TCS teams in 1988, Motorola's management was overwhelmed by the achievement of their employees. Richard Buetow, senior vice president and director of quality, said of the TCS teams' accomplishments: "We never envisioned that well-empowered people at the lowest, entry-level positions, properly trained within their skill levels, could move heaven and earth."

In the industrial age, companies squandered immense amounts of human potential on mindless, repetitive tasks and meaningless paper work. It never occurred to leaders in those days that their assembly-line workers had the know-how to go home and rebuild entire car engines, that their "lowly cashiers" easily negotiated complicated bank loans for their families, or that their "pretty little stenographers" were perfectly capable of chairing PTA meetings, managing household budgets, organizing charity drives, sitting on hospital committees, or running complex volunteer organizations in their spare time. Today, in the post-industrial information age, no company can afford to waste human capital so rashly. Every talent, every idea, every skill is needed urgently if companies are to survive in the new global economy. The potential of the work force *really is* the company's greatest asset today.

- Study your employees at work. Look for signs of boredom, restlessness, bad temper, and indifference to company goals. If you find any of those, you're not doing your job properly. People *want* to contribute, they *want* their talents stretched, and they *want* to make a difference to their colleagues and their companies. Depressed work forces aren't made up of indolent people, they're made up of underutilized people. Find means to let them do more, and they will.

- Create an environment in which employees can self-organize around workplace issues of all kinds. The Motorola competition is a fairly ritualized version of such an environment. That degree of formality may not work for your company, but there will be other ways to do it. The point is to get ideas flowing freely on the front lines.

- Be prepared to share your large-issue challenges with the whole work force. You'll be amazed how often a file clerk or a stockroom trainee will come up with a good solution you'd never have dreamed of.

- Acknowledge all contributions, useful or otherwise. Usefulness is a bonus. The important thing is to keep the contributions coming in from all sectors. Encouraging participation is one of the things that makes people feel valued, and people who feel valued are the people you want in your organization.

- Print out and pin up on your wall the following statement from John R. Black, director of lean manufacturing research and development at Boeing: "Committing wholly to the goal of relying on human potential as a central corporate strategy requires courage, ingenuity, integrity, and a passion for the human spirit. Not many companies are able to make that commitment. Fewer still are able to honor it in ways that work. But the few that manage to do *both* are enormously successful."

With one exception, success in today's global economy boils down to the single, universally recognized issue of getting more for less. The exception is human resources. The potential of an organization lies within each individual and within the connections between individuals. Human labor is no longer a disposable commodity. It is a unique creative resource for the future of the organization. You can trim production costs, speed up communications, reduce delivery times, cut corners on marketing and promotion—you can even go around the building switching off unnecessary lights the way the president of Goodyear did. But you can't switch workers off and expect to come out ahead. If you give people less, they give less back. If you treat them like underlings, they behave like underlings. Offer them more, on the other hand, and they'll repay you with interest. I'm not talking about money now. I'm talking about liberating untapped potential, about energizing employees and engaging their enthusiasm. "Better pay doesn't guarantee better performance," I always tell my audiences. "Better understanding does." Offer people a chance to grow and they will blossom. Entrust them with greater authority and they will take on greater responsibility. Educate them to understand the changing business dynamics and they will make excellent business decisions. Ask for their ideas and they will amaze you with their inventiveness and practical know-how. Treat them like full partners in the organization and they will participate like owners. Make human potential *the* corporate strategy and your company will be ready for the new business age. That, ultimately, is the moral of all the success stories I tell at conferences; a moral that today's leading companies have all learned through experience, and one that can be put to use in any company through the application of a few commonsense principles. Just take it one step at a time.

STEP 1: EXAMINE CHANGING REALITIES

- Communicate to employees the forces of change affecting markets, competition, and their jobs.
  - Acknowledge the changes in needs and values of the work force.

STEP 2: ADOPT THE NEW BUSINESS PARADIGM

- Identify the changing paradigm for science and organizations.
- Exploit instability as the opportunity for positive transformation.

STEP 3: DEVELOP A CHANGE-ADEPT WORK FORCE

- Expand employees' skills to help them thrive on change instead of fearing it.
- Develop management practices that promote change-adeptness throughout the organization.

STEP 4: LEAD DISCONTINUOUS CHANGE

- Be prepared not just to manage but to lead transformation.
- Build emotional literacy in yourself and in your work force.

STEP 5: DEVELOP THE CORE OF LEADERSHIP

- Become the change you want to see in others: Lead by example.
- Transform yourself from manager to leader.

STEP 6: RENEGOTIATE THE COMPACT BETWEEN EMPLOYERS AND EMPLOYEES

- Recognize the powerful potential of shared commitment.
- Move from paternalism to partnerships.

STEP 7: LIBERATE WORK FORCE POTENTIAL

- Eliminate obstacles to creative collaboration.
- Rely on human potential as central to your corporate strategy.

Then go back to square one and see what you have accomplished this time.

The latest restructuring is over. The work force feels safe, confident, full of energy, and eager to get on with the business at hand. Employees now realize they are part of a living system where continual change is not a threat but a mark of corporate health and personal opportunity. Anxiety has been dispelled. The ghost in the machine has been vanquished. A dynamic partnership now exists between you and your workers, and every department understands how its individual efforts contribute to the overall objectives of the organization.

Right?

A lot more likely than before, I can promise you.

But you still can't sit back and congratulate yourself on a job well done, because as a leader of change, you've changed too. In the process of energizing your employees and liberating their potential you've created a whole new kind of job for yourself, one that calls for constant effort and vigilance: a job that has no beginning or end; a job you've turned into another essential part of the living system your company has become.

"But don't worry," I always tell my audiences before I leave the platform. "You'll like who you've become. And there are some very gratifying compensations." Then I repeat something a senior manager at a leading chemical firm once told me he'd overheard in the cafeteria.

"This isn't the company I joined," one employee said to another. "It's better."

INDEX